SOCIAL SECURITY
BASIC INCOME

SOCIAL SECURITY BASIC INCOME

A Safety Net for All Americans

SECOND EDITION

Steven O. Richardson

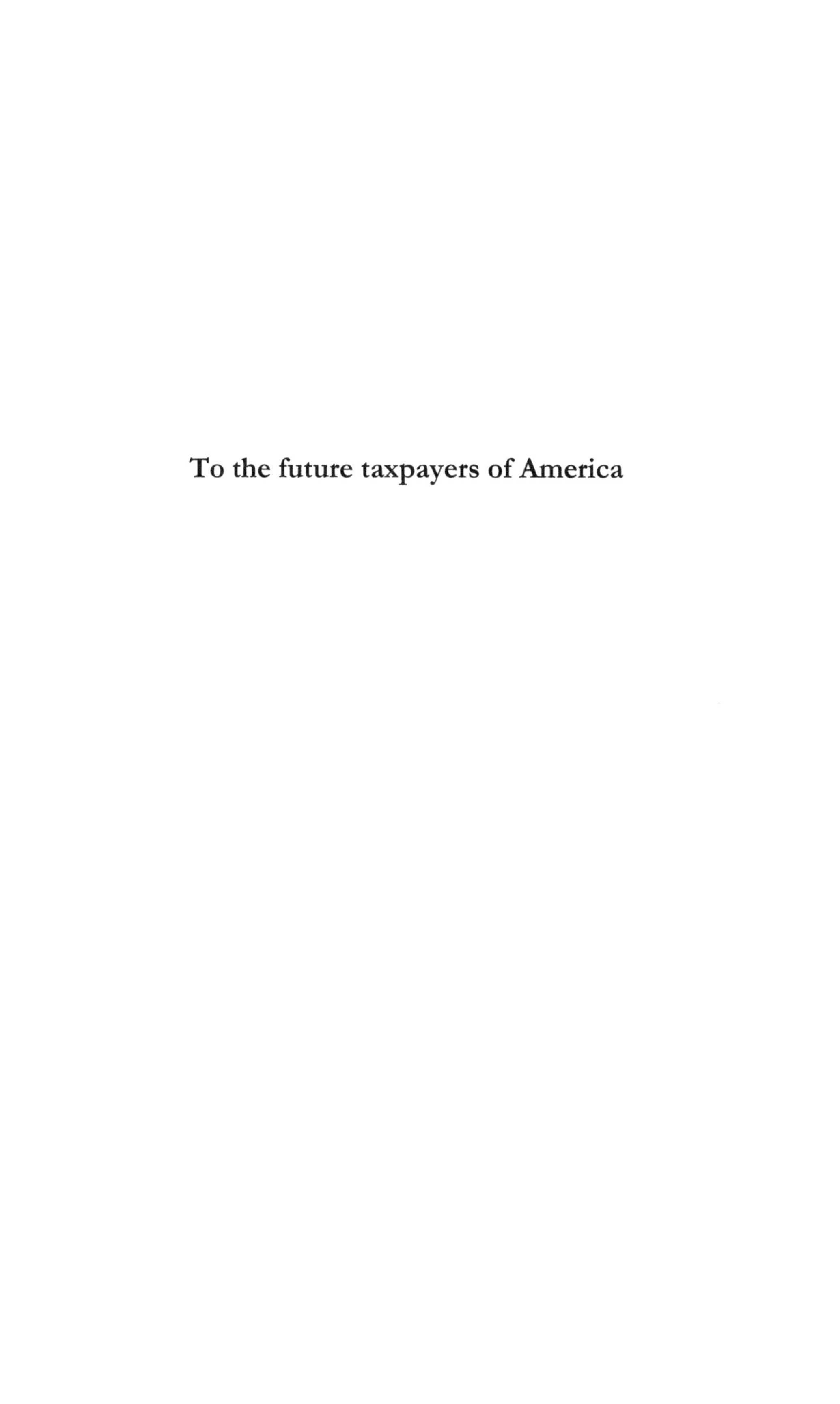

To the future taxpayers of America

Contents

Figures

Tables

Preface

If you read the first edition, you may be wondering why I'm republishing this book and how this version is different. Whether this is your first exploration of Social Security Basic Income (SSBI) or a refresher, please know that I appreciate your interest and hope you find this update encouraging, as I do.

Initial publication of this book in March 2020 coincided with pandemic shutdowns across the US and unprecedented fiscal relief in the form of the CARES Act. These events had enormous impacts on the economy. In addition, effects of the Tax Cuts and Jobs Act had not yet had time to show up in macroeconomic data. Naturally, I wondered whether design of my Free to Work (FTW) and SSBI schemes would prove robust, i.e., if calculations of revenue and program costs would hold up when those formulas were applied to more recent data.

This edition, like the first, uses the latest available data from the US Department of the Treasury, the Social Security Administration the US Department of Health and Human Services, and Office of Management and Budget sources in estimating current (status quo) tax and entitlement cash flows and comparative static analysis of how both would change for the nation and for individuals and families with various income levels and types if my policies were adopted. Most aggregate data (e.g., payroll tax revenue and Social Security benefit payments) in this edition are for Fiscal Year 2021. Tax return data needed to determine distribution profiles have more of a lag; they utilize returns for Calendar Year 2020.

Due to inflation of the Federal Poverty Guideline levels of income for individuals and families, I adjusted the basic income payment from \$1000/month to \$1250. I also increased the Child Allowance from \$4000 to \$5000 per child. I did not adjust the income surtax thresholds or levels for FTW or SSBI, nor did I adjust the SSBI surtax that phases out net payments of the basic income benefit. Nevertheless, as shown in Table 5.1, both programs are projected to improve upon the status quo in terms of paying for entitlements by several hundred billion dollars annually. For SSBI, this includes paying for legacy Social Security benefits. Figures 5.3 through 5.6 show that FTW and SSBI reforms are still projected to make federal taxes significantly more equitable (treatment of earned vs. unearned income) and more progressive (taxing higher income households more than those with lower incomes).

I have deleted a few outdated references, but more importantly, I've added and updated others, especially figures for which more recent sources were available. Table 5.1, which summarizes the features and estimated effects of both reforms, now includes Net Cost information that makes it more useful. Also, I've improved the flow of the narrative wherever I discovered such an opportunity. Names of chapters and subsections have not changed.

This book is just one concerned citizen's attempt to solve the enormous problems of income inequality and inadequacy of our largest entitlement programs. The good news is that awareness of both problems and of basic income schemes is increasing. The bad news is that the clock is running out on Social Security and Medicare trust funds, and we still have a dysfunctional Congress. My diagnosis has not changed, but needs and resources are changing quickly, so formulas and estimated effects should be revisited every few years. I am committed to keeping hope alive and keeping my proposals current so they are more likely to be considered. With any luck, a third edition will not be necessary.

Introduction

This book presents what many Americans would consider a paradox. I propose declaring independence from the system most people consider insurance and replacing it with an even larger program that looks a lot like welfare. I hope you are intrigued to see how I reconcile this apparent conflict.

The story begins with a candid look at what has become of the United States of America. I am an idealist and a patriot, but more importantly, I'm an iconoclast and a pragmatist. I care deeply about America – not the symbols and slogans but the ideas and opportunities we are privileged to share – past, present, and future. In my lifetime, they have begun to slip away, and the pace of this change is accelerating. For starters, I am obliged to explain what it is, exactly, that has me so worked up about the current state of affairs. Then I'm going to describe what I see as a way out of the mess. My goal is to persuade you that we can restore hope to many people who may be losing it.

Even as we are fed a daily diet of good news about our economy, such as record high stock market indices and record low unemployment rates, most Americans are not feeling prosperous and worry about the next recession. We also know that our country is more divided than it has been in half a century – in several dimensions. Perhaps the greatest of these divides is a large and growing income inequality, which like climate change, has achieved almost universal recognition as a serious issue that seems beyond our grasp, politically. We the People are to blame. We have allowed our democracy to become a kleptocracy. While politicians have behaved badly, their only legitimate excuse is that we elected (and re-elected) them. Our institutions have become what any reasonable person would expect, given a century or more of neglect. Using political parties as weapons of mass destruction of liberty, the ruling class has captured our government. It should be clear by now that we (the working class) will not find salvation in the system we know or in anyone who has created and defended it. We may need to reform election laws, one state at a time, before any real progress can be made on the policy front. That may be the subject of another book. In any event, regular citizens need to think for ourselves and trust one another to solve really big problems like income inequality that threaten our freedom and unity.

Federal income support revolves around Social Security, which has become a too big to fail (TBTF) program. Its solvency problems have received plenty of attention from experts, but virtually none from politicians. Consequently, it is destined for another bailout maneuver when alternatives are eliminated by the inevitable crisis. In the meantime, the concept of a Basic Income Guarantee (BIG)[1] is receiving more and more attention, primarily as a solution to automation of jobs. There are obvious connections between the issues of funding Social Security and expanding the social safety net as jobs disappear, yet even without the TBTF status of Social Security, it is too controversial and complex to attract anyone invested in an election cycle mindset. Income security and jobs are not just connected; they cannot be separated because we have joined them at the hip through payroll tax funding of Social Security and work requirements for virtually all other forms of assistance to the poor. We will not understand, analyze, or solve these problems without considering evidence and policy options from a systems perspective. Although this book proposes a very specific solution (SSBI) to the problem of income inequality, it's more importantly a plea to renew Americans' appreciation, understanding, commitment, and action to seize freedom. I don't expect anyone to agree with all of what I have to say. However, I hope everyone will find it provocative in the inspirational sense.

---

[1] Many refer to it as a Universal Basic Income (UBI) or just "basic income." I use BIG because it's a better fit with my proposal, which is unconditional and universal but structured as a negative income tax. Where I cite others, I have left their references to UBI intact.

Chapter 1. My Perspective

Before launching an exploration of fundamental ideas that influenced my analysis, I should define two terms, "ruling class" and "working class," that were used in the Introduction and will appear many more times in this book. Conservatives may assume that anyone who would use these terms is Marxist or at least progressive. I have never identified with either ideology. I'm libertarian – which is consistent with my motivation (as an idealistic patriot) even as it may make my juxtaposition of liberty and welfare confusing. My egalitarian sentiments run deep. That's why I find it unacceptable that our government so clearly favors capital at the expense of labor. While I support free markets and capitalism as a matter of principle, what I see in our country is trickle-down, supply-side economics run amok.

Consider what is implied by the shamelessly manipulative term "job creators," which is routinely used by politicians to portray employers as benefactors. It belies a smug belief that they are not only providing sustenance but making us better people, and this justifies a vast array of subsidies to businessmen. The hypocrisy of this attitude is breathtaking. In the US, welfare policies reflect the view that aid to the poor is not just undeserved but keeps them from working like they should. We make public assistance to individuals contingent on getting a job – any job. Meanwhile, in service of the noble cause of stimulating the economy, staggering amounts of money (i.e., future taxes) are manufactured by the Federal Reserve Bank (Fed) to lend to other banks and to the federal government to help businesses that could not otherwise afford to hire anyone. This is not eliminating welfare; it's a gift to rent-seekers who merely pose as capitalists.

Most of the money stays on Wall Street, which operates more and more like Las Vegas these days. New jobs that can be traced to this new money come at the expense of other jobs in less capital-intensive industries. And so it goes, as the Zero Interest Rate Policy (ZIRP) creates a zero-sum economy and Main Street resembles Las Vegas, too. The ruling class gambles with working class debt (in the form of Federal Reserve

Notes, aka dollars) limited only by the extent to which it shows up as inflation in consumer prices. In a free market economy, productivity increases lead to lower prices and higher wages, but with the Fed targeting inflation of two percent annually, gains are captured by increases in the money supply that flow through our bloated financial institutions.

Ruling class always refers to privilege and usually refers to authority. In this book it will refer to rent-seekers – people who rely on government-sanctioned advantages, usually in regulations or tax policies, including (but not limited to) corporate welfare such as tariffs and myriad corporate and individual tax deductions or credits. The working class is everyone else – rich or poor and regardless of income sources. The vast majority of those benefiting from any given policy are not easy to identify and it is impossible to know exactly which individuals (e.g., among a firm's employees, investors, and customers) are active supporters and which are passive. It doesn't really matter. I'm trying to end the class war by replacing special privileges with one universal transfer that benefits most people and bursts the bubble for some. Those who have (passively) taken advantage of random tax credits and deductions or federal programs will not celebrate their loss, but they are unlikely to actively resist. Those who have built or rescued an enterprise that relies on the status quo will be very vocal about how unfair and detrimental it is to change the rules; they will probably forecast job losses. I welcome a debate on fairness, rights, or any such claim by those who will lose advantage because I'm not advocating confiscation of past plunder – just immediate leveling of the playing field. Initially, on average, it will hurt the few more than it helps the many because it reverses policies that previously concentrated benefits and dispersed costs.

I propose eliminating most tax expenditures to pay for SSBI because they should not have been enacted in the first place. This redistribution will be characterized as welfare because it will chiefly benefit the poor, but by my definition, welfare is any form of government-funded support, and SSBI is fairly and accurately described as welfare *reform*. I'm sympathetic to the libertarian argument that taxation is theft by a tyranny of the majority. By this logic, eliminating tax expenditures is a tax increase. However, that complaint is completely undermined by another libertarian favorite: TNSTAAFL (There's No Such Thing As A Free Lunch). The principle of self-government points toward paying one's own way – not seeking exemptions. Our system is riddled with exemptions, and removing them will raise taxes on some of us. They may not agree with how much we are spending or how we are spending it. Neither do I. But that's beside the point. It's about time we restored fairness in taxation and balanced the budget. Each year presents an opportunity to revise spending priorities, and my proposal will bring entitlements (namely Social Security and Medicare) into that equation. In my view, the main thing is that we all live by the same rules, because if we do not have the rule of law – agreement to decide on rules and abide by them – we're not really American.

It's time to merge these two classes by decimating opportunities for rent-seeking and by enhancing self-government by members of the working class. SSBI is a huge step but just one example of a shift toward policies that treat everyone the same, trust people to make their own decisions, and make responsible public choices. SSBI is highly democratic. Benefits are unconditional and the terms of payment and receipt are determined through our existing legislative process. It is so simple that the only administrative functions are verification of citizenship, age, income type and amount, the number of dependent children, and payment of benefits. Citizens trust one another to spend their own stipends as they wish. The safety net is tangible evidence of egalitarianism; it implicitly recognizes the fluid nature of income in our society.

Complexity and Moral Philosophy

This book may be more comprehensible if I share a few major influences on my thinking. As mentioned in the Introduction, I am an iconoclast. Therefore, I was quite pleased to read (the year after publishing the first edition of this book) *The Dawn of Everything: A New History of Humanity*. The authors, an anthropologist and an archaeologist, questioned the axiom of social science – "a study of the ways in which human beings are not free" – that existing social orders are immutable. They lamented the loss, world-wide and over many generations, of basic freedoms to relocate, to disobey commands, and to choose or create social realities. "[T]he possibilities for human intervention are far greater than we are inclined to think." Knowledge of our past is power to reshape our conceptions of who we are and might yet become (Graeber and Wengrow 2021: 498, 502, 524-5).

Did I mention I'm an economist? Economics is the study of human action within an enormous context of living systems and a more limited history of philosophy, religion, and politics. That's why my first book, *The Political Economy of Bureaucracy*, which was also my dissertation, cited a number of sources many would not expect in a book about government (Richardson 2011). Insights of my research came from looking at the federal bureaucracy in a different way. Where others saw a machine, I saw a Kaleidic Hyperstructure[2] of semi-autonomous human beings. Understanding

---

[2] Hyperstructures are systems of systems. Kaleidic is my term for the tendency of living systems to change their structures.

the system we wish to change is critical to identifying the real problems and what might fix them. Even social scientists fall into the trap of forgetting the social part of our sciences. Major policies of all stripes are often formulated with little regard for implementation challenges, and seldom tested and revised or reversed based on evidence of effectiveness. Those that are tested fail more often than not. This does not mean interventions are bad, but it does mean we should be humble about our social engineering ambitions.

What is humble, you may ask, about proposing to rebuild the entire federal tax structure? There are a number of paradoxes in this book, some of which are enveloped in larger ones. What I am suggesting is that we have not been humble enough about public policy formulation, implementation, and assessment in the past. Understanding that is the key to appreciating how we got into the mess we're in and even more critical to getting out of it. Hubris is actually believing you have *the* answer. We all know, if we're being honest, how improbable that is even when dealing with minor problems affecting family and friends. Shouldn't we expect exponentially greater difficulty solving problems that involve millions of people?

Who am I to challenge all the Congresses, Presidents, and their most influential teachers and advisors who served us over the last century or so? I'm just one American exercising my right and responsibility to question authority. In my view, too many laws have been enacted without due diligence and allowed to do damage that could have been limited, had we been less proud. We have an unseemly habit of making monuments of our laws by naming them after politicians or catchy slogans. No one likes to admit failure and it's just as human to avoid even considering the possibility, if we can. When the subject is an act of Congress that symbolizes a hard-fought victory followed by many years of spoils (visible benefits with hidden or postponed costs), repeal is daunting at best.

What I have in mind is much bigger even than SSBI; it's changing the way we do the business of government. Politicians don't fear policy failure; they only fear losing the legislative battle. That's because we (the People) have bought one sales pitch after another and paid little attention to evidence. It's time to hold ourselves to a higher standard, i.e., to be more circumspect in taking action, more attentive to the challenges of implementation, and more interested in evidence of results. That might be possible if we have a lot fewer special interests to look after and one very important universal program to manage. Not every policy proposal needs a dissertation on morality as justification. But this one will touch every single American for generations to come, so it calls for the most thorough explanation and arguments I can muster. Whether or not SSBI is well received, I will have made an example of two ideas that could improve future federal policy debates: *systems thinking* and *agile federalism.*

Not everyone is wired to systems thinking and not every issue lends itself to such treatment. But with an undeniably complex economy and government along with fantastic technological capabilities, there is no excuse for policymaking that resembles a game of Jenga. The lifeblood of every corporate entity is its organization of resources to serve a strategy for reaching a clearly defined goal. Government entities should operate the same way, yet while we have long and short-term plans to do that, they are highly constrained by rigid control of resources and authority. These controls are designed by a Congress that lurches from one vote-buying opportunity to another. There is no glory or election campaign payoff in the painstaking work of building a complex model of the current policy landscape and determining how any given proposal would alter its configuration and operation – so no one in the policy stratosphere calls for it. How that would become routine is beyond the scope of this book, but my point is that we should seek flexible solutions that express humility regarding our own proposals.

My analysis of the complexity of phasing out Social Security and implementing a BIG acknowledges the unknowns that plague not just past policies, but my own. As complex as SSBI may appear, its chief design asset is that it can accommodate changing definitions of poverty, demographics, fiscal constraints, and individual choices. This chapter will expand upon the scientific and philosophical reasons for adopting such an approach; later chapters will demonstrate its pragmatic rationale.

While I am far from the first scholar to opine on entitlement reform, my contribution to the debate may consist mostly in daring to look at it differently. Where others see a solvency problem, I see a serous design flaw. We could raise taxes or reduce benefits for Social Security and Medicare, but doing so would miss an opportunity to solve the larger problems of poverty and inequality. Willingness to consider ambitious reform requires ditching sentimental attachments and looking at the root causes of problems we could solve if we were not hobbled by existing program structures. It also requires humble approaches to design of new solutions.

Complex adaptive systems are relatively stable because they feature fluid relationships defined by choice among component agents. In other words, they're flexible and decentralized – which is not how anyone would describe Social Security and Medicare. Both have fixed funding streams that may offer the illusion of stability. Over the long run, though, revenues have not kept up with expenditures and the degree to which both sides of that equation are tied to statute has led us into a political trap. SSBI takes the hit of grandfathering benefits earned to date but ties new benefits to the Federal Poverty Guidelines and funds them through general revenue. These key changes provide transparency and opportunities to make corrections in the annual budget process as well as through broader tax reform measures. Individual benefits are not tied to contributions or age (other than the minimum) and adjust up or down annually based on income. This flexibility is also one aspect of the ultimate decentralization of entitlements to the individual. The government guarantees a minimum level of income; payments are reduced for citizens who have earned or unearned income from other sources. The federal benefit is not adjusted to subsidize or punish choices such as where to live or whom to live with under what arrangement. The only adjustment is a child allowance modeled, like the BIG per adult, after the Federal Poverty Guidelines.

With any federal program and especially one of this size, there is a huge risk of overfishing, which is inefficient aggregate taxation caused by competition to shift costs between layers of government (Pope 2018). The most obvious example is Medicaid; states have allowed costs to rise due to federal matching funds, then the Affordable Care Act (ACA) created incentives to expand eligibility that ultimately inflate states' costs. My notion of federalism is *agile* – a flexible relationship with other levels of government in which the federal role is limited to establishing minimum protections; think Bill of Rights. I'm not sure where to draw the line between state and federal funding of health care, but flexible funding of Medicare under SSBI reforms (from the general fund instead of payroll taxes) could provide an opportunity to revisit the whole Medicare/Medicaid/ACA system. Fierce resistance to the ACA is primarily focused on the provision that forces states to design and administer programs according to federal standards. Agile federalism would operate differently; as with SSBI, we would decide on a national standard and then *fully fund and administer that program*. States that want more can supplement it however they wish – with their own tax dollars. SSBI also devolves provision of supplemental income support to state and local governments and charities by replacing other federal cash benefit programs with the universal entitlement.

Agile federalism is reflected in SSBI features that first of all cut out the middlemen (state and federal bureaucracies) wherever possible by putting cash in citizens' pockets. Not only do they avoid confusing, time-consuming, demeaning, unreliable, and inefficient administration of benefits, but beneficiaries are free to determine one dollar at a time how the money can best meet their needs. SSBI is also universal, meaning the guaranteed amount cannot be denied or augmented based on marital status, residence, or any of the other criteria we have traditionally used to discriminate.[3] The US government has hundreds of social programs that waste a great deal of money in administration and offer endless opportunities for rent-seeking. They can be replaced by one simple program that leaves it up to citizens to make adjustments. And it makes no sense as a matter of federal policy to encourage debt-financed development and then subsidize rent payments and other services that became unaffordable because of the development. People who wish to live in an expensive area or otherwise improve their living conditions may pool their resources, provided they can get along. Others may move to a more affordable area and live a simpler life instead of struggling in a place they don't like because that's where the jobs are. When everyone has access to a minimum amount of cash, options expand quickly and measurable social benefits are not limited to incomes.[4]

There is a spiritual aspect to all human relations. Public policies that affect everyone – and some profoundly – should reflect our society's values. If they are in sync, our values will be enhanced; if not, we can lose our way. About 50 years ago, the famous English Zen Buddhist Alan Watts (2015) addressed the capital/labor issue by reminding us that technology is supposed to work for us, not the other way around. He said that we have allowed 17th century Protestant myths about the devil and idleness and 20th century myths about economics to warp our thinking about work as something we all must do to earn money. As credit fueled technological growth that should have reduced the need for labor, our hang-up about everyone needing to work instead created a problem of how to keep everyone working. We created jobs "making every kind of frippery and unnecessary contraption" that we then had to convince people they need and want. As a result, people are now working for the machines. The way out, he says, is to change our attitude about money and its relationship to work – "a formidable problem."

Another powerful influence is Adam Smith's impartial spectator (Smith [1759] 1982). Academic economists have debated whether he could possibly have written *The Wealth of Nations* after *The Theory of Moral Sentiments* (TMS) because the heart in one disappeared in the other. I saw no contradiction and in fact was fascinated and delighted to discover that economics began as a moral philosophy. Exchange, in a free market, only occurs when it benefits both parties – a clear incentive to put oneself in another's shoes so as to provide the right goods under favorable terms. That's

---

[3] It is adjusted, however, by a child allowance that assists with the financial burden of raising children.

[4] Santens (2015) summarizes evidence from experiments in Namibia, India, Lebanon, North Carolina, and Alaska that show improved social cohesion (e.g., pooling resources, mutual support, and better behavior) when people receive cash with no strings attached.

exactly what TMS is about; seeking approbation of others, we judge our own actions as if we were an impartial observer and make adjustments.

Like Smith, John Rawls (1971) employs a "veil of ignorance" approach to questions of policy that have differential class-related impacts. He suggests that we can only arrive at a fair redistribution policy by imagining we had no knowledge of our own circumstances (rich or poor heritage, good or bad health, greater or lesser intelligence, etc.). If we are honest, he says, we would choose a system that maximizes our liberty while limiting public options to those that benefit the least advantaged members of society. More recent arguments that apply specifically to UBI can be traced to Philippe Van Parijs, who claimed social justice requires *unconditional* provision of public assistance (Bidadanure 2019).

Some scholars believe redistribution is a fundamental obligation of a free society. For example, where others discussed markets as a means to freedom, Amartya Sen (1999) redefined freedom in terms of access to markets. Louise Haagh (2012) suggested freedom for all requires stability in the form of Social Security funded by progressive taxation. Gregory Brazeal (2023) noted that markets are merely legal constructions; different political decisions would obviously lead to different distributions of wealth and opportunity. And Thomas Piketty (2020: 5, 7) showed that historically, income inequality reflects a society's political and property regimes: who belongs, what each person is allowed to own, and how relations between them are governed. He says:

> Inequality is neither economic nor technological; it is ideological and political.... In other words, the market and competition, profits and wages, capital and debt, skilled and unskilled workers, natives and aliens, tax havens and competitiveness – none of these things exist as such. All are social and historical constructs, which depend entirely on the legal, fiscal, educational, and political systems that people choose to adopt and the conceptual definitions they choose to work with....
>
> These choices... enable us to imagine new worlds and different types of society.

These ideas, all of which emphasize unnatural selection at play, inspired Chapter 4 – a moral inventory of federal policies that bear on entitlement reform. Despite my distaste for coercive redistribution, I became convinced that it was necessary to amend past policy mistakes that caused chronic income inequality.

As I will explain in some detail, the worst of our errors in the last 50 years involved subsidizing capital at the expense of labor. Using the monopoly power of a central bank to suppress interest rates, we reduced the cost of borrowing for those with access to credit while inflating away the purchasing power of wages. We may never be able to correct these huge monetary policy mistakes. Fiscal policy is a mess, too, but it is more easily corrected. SSBI is a blunt instrument that will eliminate some of the most harmful provisions of the tax code and immediately improve options for low-income individuals and families. It should buy us some time to work on more nuanced aspects of policy and look into options that might create a free market for money.

Fiscally Responsible Welfare

The good news is that our biggest challenge is not creating wealth but distributing it. Theoretically, we can satisfy a Rawlsian condition of fairness by redistribution.[5] The problem is that in the US, capitalism has become a religion that abhors social welfare even as financial market worshipers are thriving thanks to corporate welfare. Capitalists with access to funding have become our "job creators" – the only source of a decent income for most of us. "Earned" credentials allow us to compete for the privilege of "earning" income. Losers in the job lottery (with or without credentials) experience not just financial insecurity but shame in a society that is largely contemptuous of the unemployed. Culturally, we disapprove of entitlements, but we make an exception for Social Security because it employs a clever device: *earned* benefits. This insidious term has turned otherwise charitable people into hypocrites. Entitlement is in the eye of the beholder. Relatively wealthy beneficiaries look down upon poor people who are dependent on other forms of welfare, as if to say: "Mine is earned, while yours is undeserved."

Federal policies that favor the one percent add insult to injury through barely concealed suggestions that the poor are a burden. We have attempted to remove the stigma by, for example, replacing food stamps with debit cards. However, we have avoided scrutiny of the systematic extortion of public funds by those who can afford large campaign contributions and lobbyists. Very few of the 99 percent have had it easy, so it's tempting to believe the poor can and should earn their way into the middle class (like the rest of us). Those who have given up or never really had a chance are blamed for the high cost of medical care, crime, and education. Complaints from or on behalf of the poor about living conditions and civil rights violations are an affront to the narrative that our hard work pays the taxes that support them. We are loath to admit that personal income taxes don't even cover public services to the middle class, never mind the poor. We should know better than to think that those with the least capabilities are responsible for others' far more manageable disappointments and

---

[5] Rawls' difference principle focuses on improving expectations of the least advantaged members of society (Rawls 1971: 68-9).

struggles. Because they are needy and powerless, the poor make easy targets for middle class resentment, but it's mean and shortsighted to scorn dependents when we have created a system that perpetuates dependency.

That doesn't mean we have to sign a blank check to show compassion; it means taking responsibility for fixing what's wrong with our system. Yuval Levin (2014) thinks we need to take a close look at individuals' relation to the state: "Moral individualism mixed with economic collectivism feels like freedom only because it liberates people from responsibility in both arenas. But real freedom is possible only with real responsibility." He takes issue with the idea that government can design and administer effective social programs – preferring instead dispersion of control because knowledge of both problems and feasible solutions is dispersed (local). As indicated in the preceding section, I strongly support structural decentralization of power, or federalism, not just because it is more efficient but because it is better for human development. SSBI is enormous and with it would come risks and challenges at an unprecedented scale. However, it should become clear as we proceed to explore the details that SSBI will simplify the federal role in social welfare. Its most significant effects would occur at the state level as governors and legislatures debate how to adjust the taxes and social services they control. Putting money in people's hands cuts more red tape than any policy analyst or official could imagine.

Social Security and Medicare benefit payments, which total almost $2 trillion annually, have for many years been among the largest federal outlays (US OMB 2023: Table 8.5). Both are classified as mandatory expenditures, meaning they are not subject to Congressional appropriations. This is symbolically important reassurance to those who have been promised assistance, and it's practical, because distributions are made by formula. But it also helps lawmakers avoid difficult choices that would accompany annual review of their budgets if they had to adjust both programs' funding and benefits along with responsibility to balance the federal budget. The arrangement has allowed Congress to bicker over discretionary budgets that concern special interests while ignoring solvency issues that affect virtually every American.

These mandatory budgets are a problem because the dedicated funding source (payroll taxes) is very difficult to change and growing benefit payments are contributing to annual budget deficits that now routinely exceed one trillion dollars. If spending was limited to revenues or if revenues were actually set aside for participants, it might make sense to have a separate, dedicated funding source. However, the taxes are fixed even while collections are commingled with income tax and other general revenue. The cost of maintaining the façade of "contributions" funding benefit payments has become untenable. We need flexibility – to raise revenues, reduce benefits, and even to change the sources of funding and terms of eligibility – because as currently structured, these programs increase inequality. Also, it's high time we explicitly recognized them as welfare programs. This would put a spotlight on the folly of funding them with a regressive tax on low-wage workers. If we have any intention of helping the working poor, we should first of all get government off of their backs by eliminating the payroll tax. Another reason to pay benefits from current revenue is to better secure workers' financial future. Of course, nothing we do with budgets for Social Security and Medicare will matter if general revenues and expenditures are not balanced. Let Members of Congress exercise their beloved power of the purse in a responsible manner by demonstrating the priority of aid to the poor with offsets from other budget items.

I propose to gradually replace existing "earned" Social Security benefits with a new negative income tax type guaranteed income tied to the official Federal Poverty Guidelines (currently about $1250 per month for an individual); monthly payments will be recalculated annually to adjust for changes in incomes as well as official poverty levels. Changing the way these programs are financed will provide flexibility needed to improve their effectiveness and fiscal integrity. Naturally, those heavily invested in Social Security may feel threatened by such radical changes. But we owe it to future generations to keep special interests from preventing responsible choices. We can and should make good on promises made to date and enter good faith negotiation of new benefit formulas. This is what our democratic process is supposed to do – engage citizens in public debate of policy options. Ideally, budgets will no longer sidestep entitlements altogether but instead confirm or revise critical funding and distribution formulas. If we question whether elected representatives are looking out for our interests or suspect they are paying lip service to us while they do the bidding of campaign contributors and party bosses, we can vote accordingly.

Those dependent on payments or tax breaks (and Congress has sought to place most of us into one or both categories) want them to continue and therefore, have not been interested in transparency. Those paying for but not yet enjoying the benefits are too busy working to demand something better and probably see no chance of winning a fight against payroll taxes. And of course, most of it is not being paid for at all; it's on the tab that will be presented to citizens not yet old enough to vote or not yet born.

Call me old-fashioned, but in my view, this is dereliction of duty. Our leaders are trusted to use their innate ability, resources, and power to make decisions better for us than those we are otherwise capable of making. Patronizing justification of irresponsible practices (e.g., blaming the voters) does not inspire confidence; it earns approval ratings of about 20 percent (RealClear Politics 2023). Of course, most of us want to have our cake and eat it, too. But we need to hear "No" just as much as children need parents to say so – and to teach by example sincerity, integrity, restraint, prudence, wisdom, compromise, humility, trust, resilience, etc. It doesn't take a political science degree to understand that representative government will not work if representatives merely convene to grant everyone's wishes by pretending that rules we live by individually do not apply to collective choices. No wonder millions of us are just a few paychecks from bankruptcy and our go-to solution for seemingly every problem is more government. John F. Kennedy must be spinning in his grave.

Don't get me wrong. I've given up the libertarian fantasy that we can all fend for ourselves or rely on charity. The federal government will always have a legitimate and very important role to play in protecting public safety and health. In fact, as I argue in this book, it is not doing enough. Treating Social Security and Medicare as sacred cows has not protected the people they are supposed to help; it has precluded consideration of more suitable alternatives. One major problem with Social Security in particular is the way it has created entitlements. I'll discuss this further in Chapter 5, but at this point I'd like to focus on the difference between perception and reality. I've just claimed that it is the job of our representatives – presumably the grown-ups – to advocate for realism in what we can and should expect from government. This suggests we do the dreaming and they say it's not real. Yet in the case of Social Security, they say it's real and leave it to some future generation to discover it was just a dream. Unlike Social Security, whereby what I pay in today creates an obligation of the government to pay me something up to 50 years later, SSBI is reality-based. It features annual payments of benefits based on current income.

Chapter 2. What's the Problem?

Moral outrage is insufficient justification for change. This chapter demonstrates that
I take seriously the responsibility of presenting evidence not only of what I find
unacceptable about the current state of affairs, but what I believe are its causes. Most
of it will be familiar to anyone interested in this book, but hopefully, readers will find
it presented in a unique, coherent, and compelling way that inspires action.

American exceptionalism as I perceive it is the belief that we are great because we
are Americans and that what we do is great because we are doing it. I think we have
rested on our laurels to a very dangerous extent. For the last 100 years, we have been
first among nations by many measures of prosperity and we have enjoyed dominant
power and influence. Not all nations have appreciated the way we've obtained and
exercised our "greatness." My concern is that, like other great empires of yore, we
have become our own worst enemy by focusing on conquest at the expense of
protecting and enriching what made us great in the first place.

Global dominance by the US and impressive aggregate measures of prosperity
such as GDP, stock market capitalization, and average income levels hide the fact that
most Americans share the burdens but not the rewards implied by these statistics.
GDP measures production, not national welfare.[6] Record low national
unemployment rates have been cited as evidence of economic health and plentiful
jobs, even though the measures exclude people who have lost hope and quit looking
for work. And to make matters worse, all jobs are counted the same, regardless of
hours worked or wages paid. Unfortunately, labor statistics have become measures
of gifts from the "job creators" to workers. Symptoms of the national malaise include
1) increasing income inequality and capital/income shares, 2) unequal income

---

[6] To increase awareness of the unequal distribution of national income, Heather Boushey
(2019a: 198-203) proposes publication of a disaggregated measure, the percentage of per-
capita annual income growth flowing to the bottom 50 percent, the next 40 percent, the top
10 percent, and the top 1 percent.

distribution in the US vs. other developed nations, and 3) alarming levels of income redistribution from younger to older Americans. SSBI would treat those symptoms to revive our spirit. However, it is far more likely that we would need a revival first, because SSBI is a virtual about face from policies that have trended in the opposite direction for generations.

I think we all know what is wrong (and thank God for that, because therein lies hope). Whether we read, watch, or listen to the news, we are all witnessing a crisis of our democratic system that has unique features but has been compared to the dark days of Vietnam and Watergate over fifty years ago, when trust in our leaders and in each other were disturbingly low. Polarization and isolation into red and blue, black and white, US-born and immigrant, old and young, and even male and female has reached dangerous levels. These, too, are symptoms of our individual, collective, and cumulative choices to outsource government. I believe the solution lies in restoring self-government. Our system was designed to help us decide on a limited number of rules to guide our behavior. But today, some of us hire or elect political mercenaries to carve out specific advantages while the rest sit out the sausage-making. Ugliness and complexity become self-reinforcing as those who thrive on it prosper and others look for the exits. This is how we got declining voter participation rates and more voters choosing independent status than affiliation with either major party, despite its disadvantages (US Census Bureau 2021, Gallup 2023).

If we are not already numb to tribalism, we can seize control of our government from the parasitic professionals and their crony capitalist patrons and insist on a universal safety net that immediately and dramatically addresses extreme income inequality. If we do not act soon, things could get much worse.

Growing Insecurity and Inequality

Although six in 10 retired adults report that Social Security is a major source of their income, barely one third of those not yet retired believe it will be for them (Brenan 2023). Yet savings for this group do not appear to be on track to make up the difference. Among households with retirement accounts, the median balance in 2019 was just $134,000 for those with a reference person (formerly "head") aged 55-64 (Federal Reserve Board 2021b). They may be able to work longer, but there is no denying that workers are getting no help from an economy in which real wages have hardly budged since 1979 (US Department of Labor, Bureau of Labor Statistics 2023b).

As indicated in Figure 2.1, before 1980 the poor fared better than the middle class and wealthier individuals on an after-tax basis. Since then, even after paying taxes, richer Americans have seen their income grow much faster than the poor, whose income hardly grew at all. According to Piketty, Saez, and Zucman (2018: 581-4), "Perhaps the most striking development in the U.S. economy over the past decades is the stagnation of income in the bottom 50%.... [A]ll the growth in posttax bottom 50% income owes to the increase in income for the elderly. For the working-age population, posttax bottom 50% income has hardly increased since 1980."

Figure 2.1 Income inequality unabated since 1980

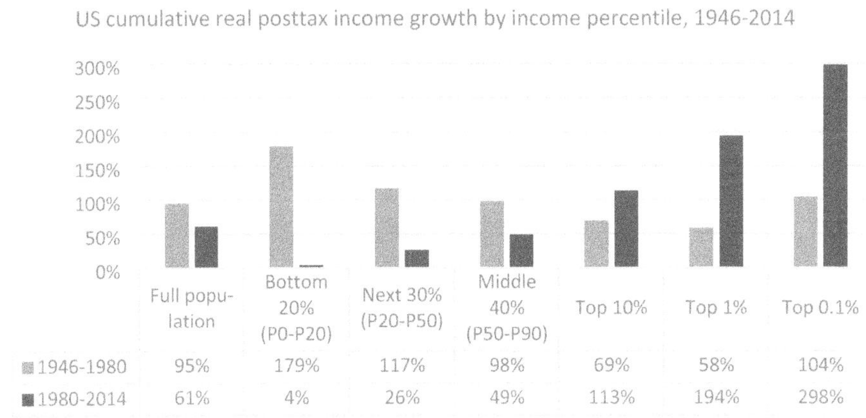

Source: Piketty, Saez, and Zucman 2018: 578

Figure 2.2 (Boushey 2019b) uses the same data to compare income growth rates by percentile to their averages before and after 1980. In her testimony before Congress, Heather Boushey of the Washington Center for Equitable Growth says, "GDP growth has been treated for decades by pundits and policymakers alike as synonymous with prosperity. President John. F. Kennedy famously alluded to it when he said that 'a rising tide lifts all boats.' In the decades since, economists and commentators have used the metaphor of 'growing the pie' to indicate that we should first and foremost be concerned with growing the economy rather than concerning ourselves with who gets a slice. But as [the figure] demonstrates, overall growth of the economic pie is no longer correlated with prosperity for many Americans."

Figure 2.2 Reversal of fortunes

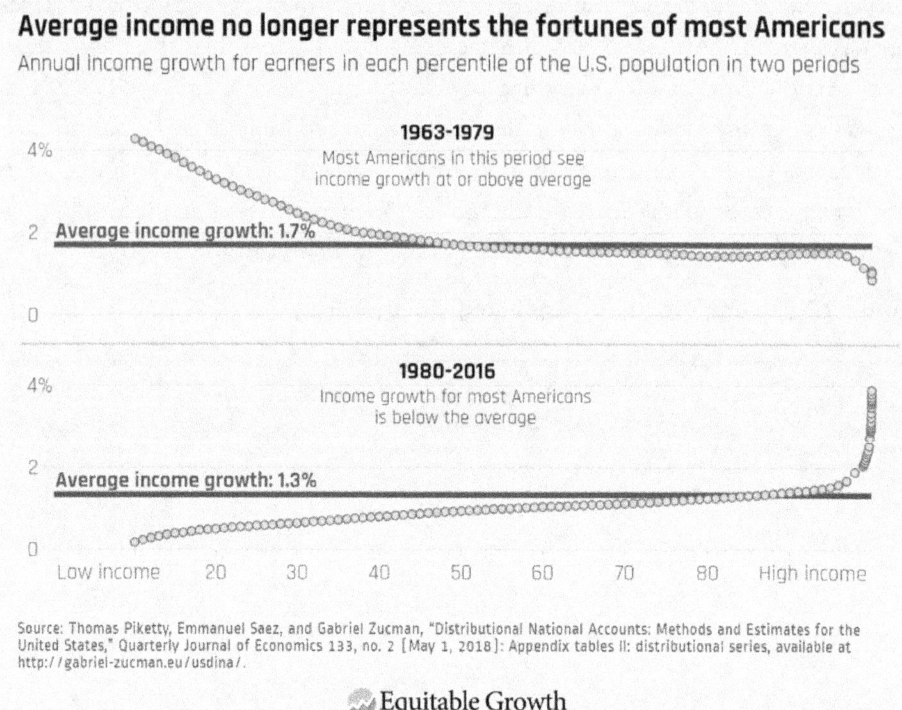

Source: Thomas Piketty, Emmanuel Saez, and Gabriel Zucman, "Distributional National Accounts: Methods and Estimates for the United States," Quarterly Journal of Economics 133, no. 2 [May 1, 2018]: Appendix tables II: distributional series, available at http://gabriel-zucman.eu/usdina/.

Equitable Growth

According to the Federal Reserve's triennial Survey of Consumer Finances (as shown in Figure 2.3, "The top 1 percent of families now receives nearly as large a share of total income as the next highest 9 percent of families combined (percentiles 91 through 99), who received 26.5 percent of all income. This share has remained fairly stable over the past quarter of a century. Correspondingly, the rising income share of the top 1 percent mirrors the declining income share of the bottom 90 percent of the distribution, which fell to 49.7 percent in 2016" (Bricker et al. 2017: 10).

Figure 2.3 Top 1% income gains come at expense of bottom 90%

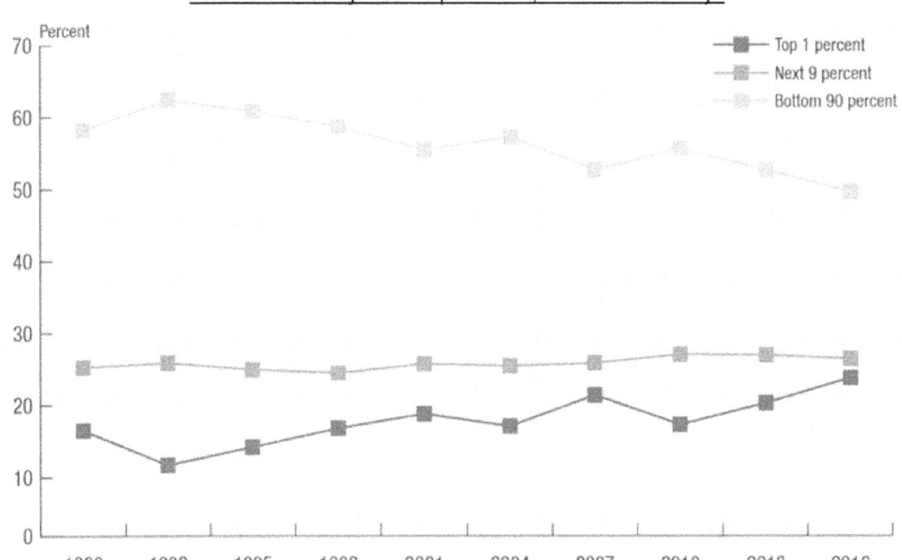

And consider this conclusion of the United Nations Human Rights Council (UNHRC):

[America's] immense wealth and expertise stand in shocking contrast with the conditions in which vast numbers of its citizens live. About 40 million live in poverty, 18.5 million in extreme poverty, and 5.3 million live in Third World conditions of absolute poverty. It has the highest youth poverty rate in the Organization for Economic Cooperation and Development (OECD), and the highest infant mortality rates among comparable OECD States. Its citizens live shorter and sicker lives compared to those living in all other rich democracies, eradicable tropical diseases are increasingly prevalent, and it has the world's highest incarceration rate, one of the lowest levels of voter registrations in among OECD countries and the highest obesity levels in the developed world. The United States has the highest rate of income inequality among Western countries…. The United States has one of the highest poverty and inequality levels among the OECD countries, and the Stanford Center on Inequality and Poverty ranks it 18th out of 21 wealthy countries in terms of labour markets, poverty rates, safety nets, wealth inequality and economic mobility. But in 2018 the United States had over 25 per cent of the world's 2,208 billionaires. There is thus a dramatic contrast between the immense wealth of the few and the squalor and deprivation in which vast numbers of Americans exist (Alston 2018: 3-4).

One of the reasons for stagnant wages is investments in technology have come at the expense of labor. For almost half a century, corporate profits have grown as wages declined, measured as shares of GDP. And it's not over yet; half of all jobs remain at risk of automation (Hughes 2014). Further in this chapter I cite unnecessary subsidies of capital investment via monetary and tax policy. But even without that help, the productivity of technology may be greater than similar investments in labor, in which case we need to face the difficult choice of what to do about structural unemployment. Protecting, redistributing, and creating employment are not good solutions because they are economically inefficient; attempts to slow progress will punish consumers and weaken competitiveness without affecting the long-term trend.[7] Education is not the answer, either, because it merely accelerates displacement of less skilled workers. The simple solution is to let innovation flourish while considering how to fairly distribute the wealth it creates. Hughes concludes, "Today the growing signs of technological unemployment and the gathering old-age dependency crisis are creating the material preconditions for campaigns for a BIG. The BIG proposal offers a way to fundamentally renegotiate the Social Security and pension system, progressive taxation and the Earned Income Tax Credit, the retirement age, and disability and unemployment insurance in a way that is attractive, for different reasons, to progressives, libertarians and fiscal conservatives."[8]

Equitable funding of any basic income scheme is bound to require highly progressive taxation. It's easy to target the one percenters, but the math doesn't work, so any real solution is going to cut far more deeply into the wealth and income distributions. While my proposal seeks to undo the worst tax policies, it is hardly based on a presumption that wealth and high incomes are ill-gotten. Nevertheless, we can count on strong protests that net beneficiaries of an income guarantee do not deserve others' earnings. I'm sympathetic but offer in response insights provided by Matthew Stewart (2018) in a brilliant article on our relatively new meritocratic class, "the 9.9 percent," who "are not innocent bystanders to the growing concentration of wealth in our time." Stewart is concerned about decreasing mobility, as measured by IGE (intergenerational earnings elasticity), from under 0.3 to about 0.5. This means earnings are increasingly determined by parents' incomes.[9] Why? The main factors are education advantages (which work in tandem with technology-driven unemployment), lower tax rates than the 90 percent (when deductions, payroll and

---

[7] Workers threatened by technology will disagree and may have the political power to enact these suboptimal solutions. This is already happening with trade policy.

[8] The public is evenly divided on this issue (Reinhart 2018).

[9] See also Mitnik and Grusky (2015).

sales taxes are included), and inflation of real estate and other assets. The privileged do not feel privileged because statistically, they have not increased their share of the national wealth; they "are the staff that runs the machine that funnels resources from the 90 percent to the 0.1 percent." This breeds resentment that led to Trump's election and continues to fuel political divisions. Stewart concludes, "The defining challenge of our time is to renew the promise of American democracy by reversing the calcifying effects of accelerating inequality. As long as inequality rules, reason will be absent from our politics; without reason, none of our other issues can be solved."

Elizabeth Kolbert (2018) shared an insight on the social cost of inequality – that people who earn less feel poor while those earning more do not feel much better. The poor engage in riskier behavior as an unhealthy reaction to feeling poor, which just keeps them poor. And the affluent do not feel good because they tend to compare their lot to those doing much better, in part to feel less guilty about their affluence. She concludes that we need to pay less attention to generating wealth and more to how it is distributed.

Poverty is defined by Matthew Desmond (2023: 13-23, 95-9) as "pain, … instability, … constant fear, … loss of liberty, … embarrassing, … and diminished life and personhood." Americans are all responsible for allowing these living conditions to develop and persist, he says, because we exhibit or tolerate contempt for the poor. Hypocritically, we endorse policies that give the most help to those who need it least while blaming the poor for their dependency on public assistance. This is because "middle- and upper-class Americans believe they – but not the poor – are entitled to government help."

Daniel Markovits (2019: 27, 72, 96, 187-8, 266-8) developed a theory that meritocracy has created a self-reinforcing cycle of reward, privilege, and education that harms the middle class more than it helps the rich because elites invent new technologies that make "the best jobs better and all other jobs worse." The value of the new jobs is contingent on a financialized economy that is fundamentally reliant on economic inequality. While merit determines success among elites, it also excludes everyone else. Middle-class jobs are increasingly "gloomy jobs – subject to intrusive, nerve-wracking, and degrading surveillance and control" that deprive workers of dignity. Work used to instill pride and hope, but in today's meritocracy, more often it brings frustration to those who cannot qualify for more rewarding jobs.

Capital is far more flexible than labor; this explains why its advantage has led to steady substitution over hundreds of years – a trend that shows no signs of slowing. Couple this with the fact that capital is always more unequally distributed than labor, and increasing inequality of wealth and income is no mystery (Piketty 2017: 277-9,

305-6). Figure 2.4 shows that capital income absorbed between 15 and 25 percent of national income in rich countries in 1970, and between 25 and 30 percent in 2010.

Figure 2.4 Rapid worldwide growth in capital/income ratios

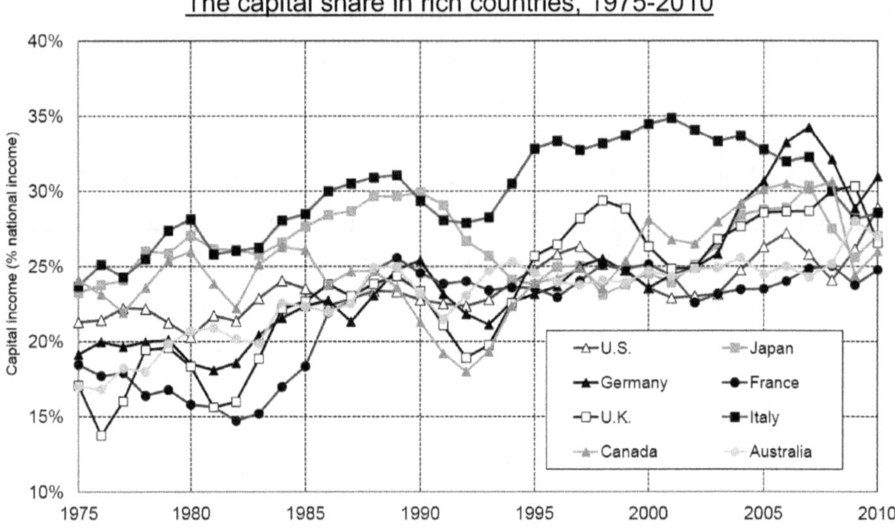

Source: Piketty 2017: 278

We do not know whether there is an ideal ratio of capital to national income. What we do know is that in recent decades, the US has managed to accelerate the process. Thomas Piketty (2017: 373) sees nothing to prevent continuation of this trend and expresses concern, with references to Karl Marx, that capitalism may undermine itself by provoking revolution.

[F]rom 1977 to 2007, we find that the richest 10 percent appropriated three-quarters of the growth. The richest 1 percent alone absorbed nearly 60 percent of the total increase in national income in this period. Hence for the bottom 90 percent, the rate of income growth was less than 0.5 percent per year. These figures are incontestable, and they are striking; whatever one thinks about the fundamental legitimacy of income inequality, the numbers deserve closer scrutiny. It is hard to imagine an economy and society that can continue functioning indefinitely with such extreme divergence between social groups.

Unsurprisingly, most entitlement reform ideas take the existing structure of flawed programs as given and propose tweaks that might appeal to Congress. For example, a report published by the American Enterprise Institute (AEI) lists a couple of dozen safety net reforms such as block grants to replace federal income support programs, Earned Income Tax Credits (EITC), Supplemental Nutrition Assistance Program

(SNAP), Temporary Assistance to Needy Families (TANF), and child support enforcement that promote work (Biggs et al. 2016: 5-6). In other words, they recommend doubling down on the strategy that has failed.

By contrast, the aforementioned UNHRC report slams a number of US policies that it claims mire unfortunate Americans in a quicksand of poverty. The critique includes disenfranchisement of minorities, discriminatory mistrust of the poor, inadequate health care, criminalization of the homeless, justice system fines and fees, and punitive drug abuse policies. It also challenges the assumption that jobs are available to the poor that can make them independent (Alston 2018: 7-17).

Shaefer and Edin (2018: 25-6, italics added) found that the drastic reductions in cash assistance following welfare reform in the '90s pushed thousands of children into extreme poverty, especially those in single-mother households. "In 1995, some 289,000 SNAP households with children reported *no source of cash income*. That number began to rise in 2002, and by 2005 it had jumped to about 599,000. By 2015, this figure had grown to just under 1.3 million, down slightly from 2014."

The supply side economic argument that policies favoring wealth creation also benefit the poor is contradicted by time series data I have already presented. In addition, the chart below suggests that our economy behaves very differently from other comparable countries. We have the highest poverty rate and by far the highest percentage of income flowing to the top one percent. While no one is likely to be surprised that the richest Americans manage to capture the largest share of incomes, it may be surprising to learn that their gains do not benefit those at the lower end of the income distribution. If they were really creating good jobs through investing their wealth, one would expect to see the US in the lower right quadrant of the chart with Switzerland, whose poverty rate is below the median even though their top 1 percent capture more of national income than the median developed country.

Figure 2.5 Relative poverty and top income shares

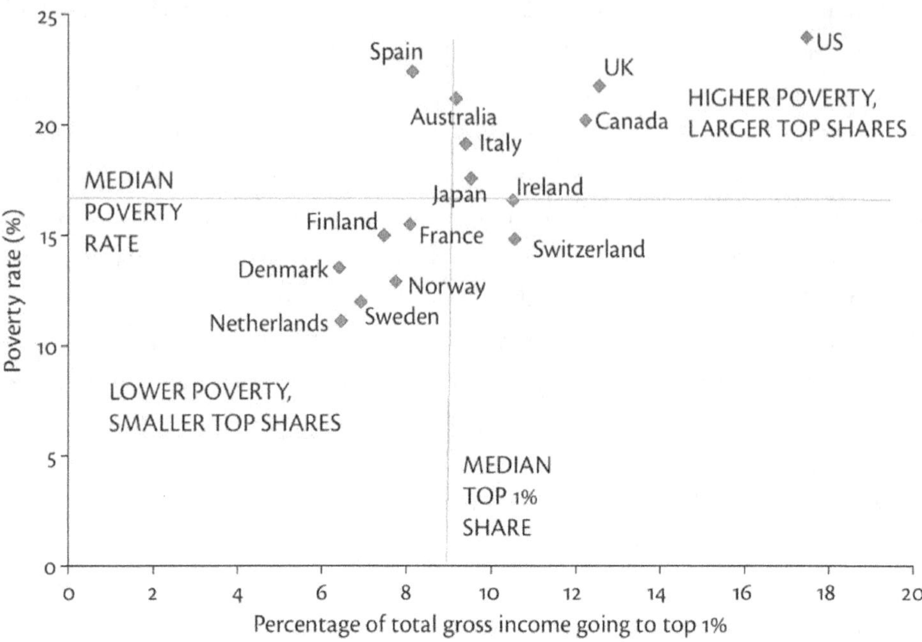

In the US in 2010 the relative poverty rate (percentage living on incomes below 60 per cent of the median) was 24.7 percent and the share of total gross income going to the top 1 percent (excluding capital gains) was 17.5 percent (Atkinson 2015: 26).

This isn't just earning power at work. As indicated in Figure 2.6 (Barnes et al. 2021: 15), policy choices take the US from #10 on a ranking of pre-tax income inequality among developed nations to #1 on an after-tax basis.[10]

---

[10] The Gini coefficient is a coefficient of income inequality on a scale from 0 to 1. A country in which everyone has the same income would have a Gini coefficient of 0, while a country in which one person earned all the income and everyone else had no income would have a Gini coefficient of 1.

Figure 2.6 Policies make US #1 in income inequality

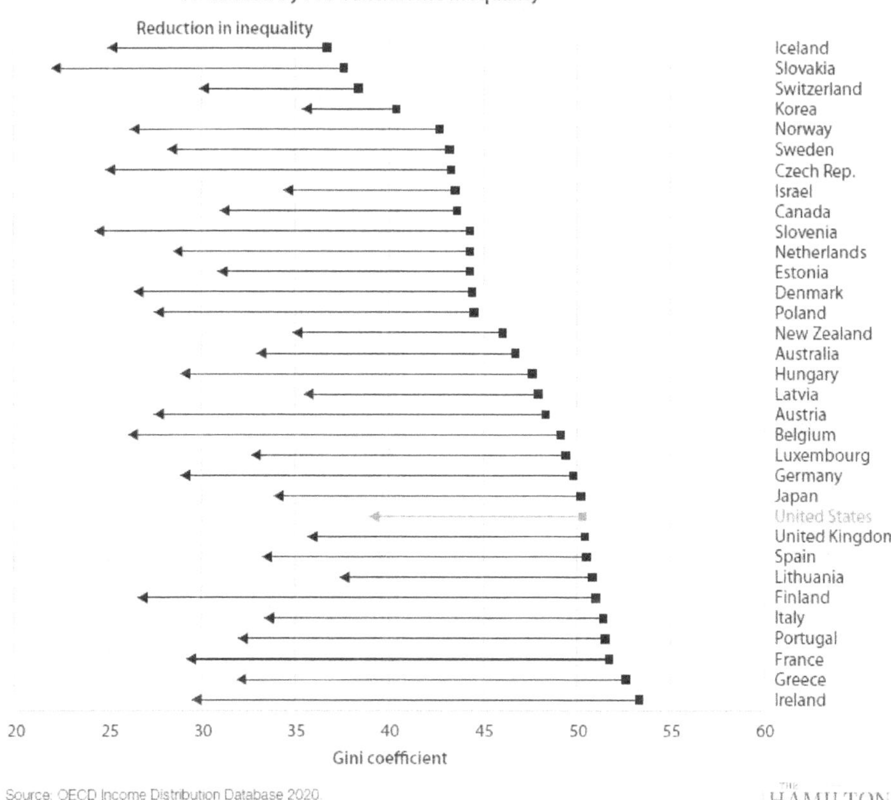

Middle-class workers are suffering, too, from lack of opportunity and income insecurity. Women make up far more of the workforce today than they did a few generations ago. However, progress on gender equality may have contributed to rising income inequality. Since the late 1970s, women's gains have largely been offset by men's losses in earnings, and high-earning men and women tend to marry one another. For those without college degrees, marriage rates fell as divorce rates rose (Coontz 2014). As shown in Figure 2.7 (US Census Bureau 2022b), as the number of workers grew by 55 percent (since 1980), median household incomes grew by just 22 percent while mean incomes grew by 44 percent. The growth differential between the number of earners and the median income indicates more workers are needed to maintain moderate household incomes. The growth differential between the median and mean incomes indicates that for high earners, household income has grown proportionally to the number of people working. Whatever the cause, it is further evidence of growing income inequality.

Figure 2.7 Middle class struggles to keep up

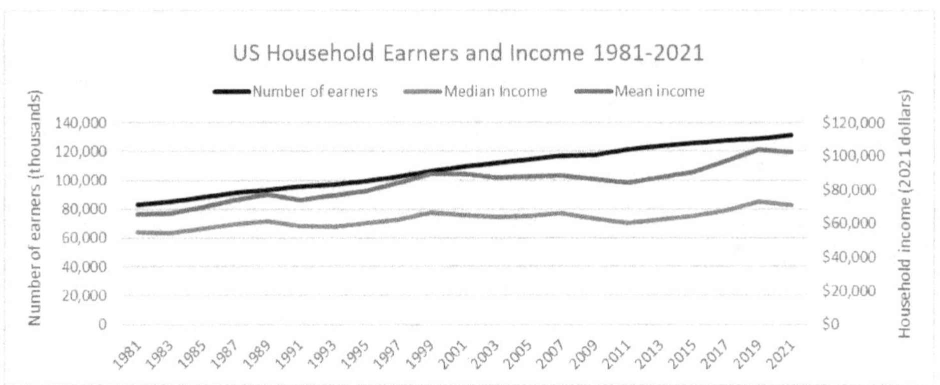

Growth in household incomes is unequal because, over the last three decades, jobs offer increasingly fewer working hours at lower relative wages. Service sector employment, which was 58 percent of all private sector employment in the 1960s, grew to 83 percent in the Great Recession, where it has remained since – indicating "peak" service employment. Service sector jobs have, also since the 1960s, paid much less than goods-producing jobs. In the decade ending in 2018, the ratio of weekly earnings for production and non-supervisory service sector employees to those in goods-producing sector was just under 75 percent (Alpert et al. 2019: 5-10).

Fifty years ago, poor and middle-class Americans assumed each generation would prosper compared to their parents. Yet by 2009, the US had one of the lowest rates of intergenerational economic mobility among wealthy democratic countries (Autor, Mindell, and Reynolds 2019: 16). And, as indicated in Figure 2.8 (Federal Reserve Board 2021a), real incomes of American households whose reference person (formerly "head") is 65 or older increased by over 50 percent from 1989 to 2019. Meanwhile, for those under 35 or 55-64, the increase was about 20 percent, and for those 35-54, incomes were flat.

Figure 2.8 Older families prosper while the young struggle

<u>Before-tax family income (thousands of 2019 dollars) by age of reference person</u>

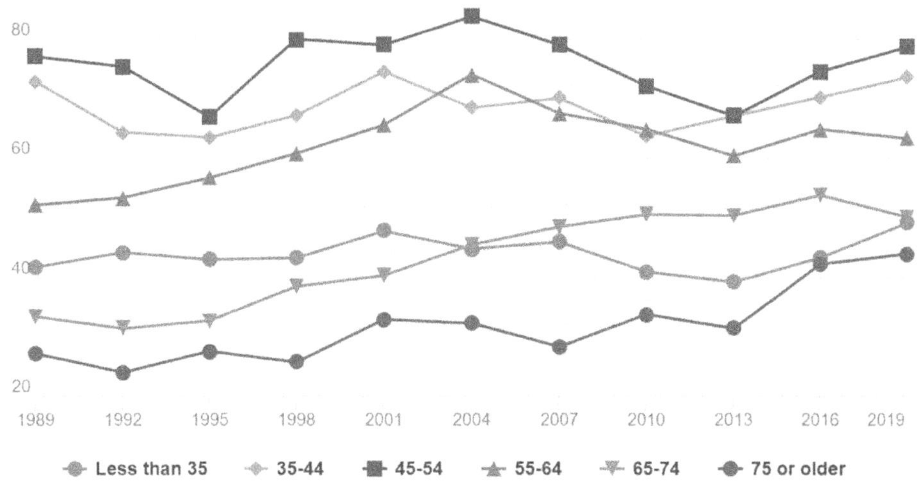

I would expect earnings to increase with age until retirement and then decline, which is exactly what the relative levels in the chart tell us – in 1989. Incomes nearly double as we move from the under 35 group to the next age group, and then they rise slightly in what is known as the peak earning years of 45-55. In that era, most workers were retired by age 65, so it is no surprise that earnings fell sharply for the next age group and even further for the 65-74 group, in which few remained in the workforce. By 75, virtually everyone was living on pensions, savings, Social Security, and other unearned income sources.

By 2019, the data tell a very different story. The most obvious difference is that the range narrowed from almost $50,000 per year to less than $35,000. In 1989, the median under 35 household income was 54 percent higher than the median 75 or older household, but by 2019 the gap had narrowed to less than 12 percent. Incomes of age 65-74 households caught up with the under 35 group. In 1989, their median income was 80 percent as high; in 2019, the same ratio was 102 percent. Hooray for older households that are doing well due to thrift and prudent investment, but for many of them, there is no question that at least some of their relative prosperity is due to payroll taxes levied on younger workers.

Households in their prime earning years (35-54) barely kept up with inflation in the 30-year period. Meanwhile, median income for the age 55-64 households increased from $51,900 to $63,120. The older cohort includes a significant number of retired persons, but fewer in 2019 than in 1989, relatively speaking. Again, the good news for older workers comes at the expense of workers in their prime.

Milton Friedman (1962: 184, 191) said of Social Security) over fifty years ago, "I do not see any grounds – liberal or other – on which this particular redistribution can be defended. The subsidy to the beneficiaries is independent of their poverty or wealth; the man of means receives it as much as the indigent. The tax which pays the subsidy is a flat-rate tax on earnings up to a maximum. It constitutes a larger fraction of low incomes than of high. What conceivable justification is there for taxing the young to subsidize the old regardless of the economic status of the old; for imposing a higher rate of tax for this purpose on the low incomes than on the high; or, for that matter, for raising the revenues to pay the subsidy by a tax on payrolls?" A program aimed at poverty relief "should be designed to help people not as members of particular occupational groups or age groups or wage-rate groups or labor organizations or industries." Especially with our aging population, it is vital that we shift to general funding of Social Security benefits and revise distribution formulas. SSBI would make the safety net available to all who need it, with benchmarks at the Federal Poverty Guidelines and eligibility at 18 instead of 62.

Inflation and a Legacy of Debt

SSBI transfers and funding mechanisms (eliminating tax expenditures and more progressive income taxes) may reduce absolute measures of inequality. However, fiscal policy is no match for the power to print wielded by our central bank – and the fact that it is and always will be controlled by the ruling class. Eliminate the bank and we may have a chance of eliminating the ruling class (not the people, of course, just the ruling part). I cannot do justice to the subject here, but the Fed's role cannot be ignored, so I'm going to delve into the macroeconomic context.

US monetary policy is a plague on citizens with lower- and middle-class incomes. Artificially low interest rates have inflated the value of assets at the expense of real wages. This has clearly aided the wealthy as it impoverished the 90 percent of Americans whose savings earn nothing and whose wages are not keeping up with inflation of housing, education, and health expenses. As we will see, this is not a bug but a feature of the system.

Figures 2.9 and 2.10 indicate how increases in M3, the broadest measure of money supply, have affected the dollar's value. Figure 2.9 (Organization for Economic Cooperation and Development 2023) shows that M3 grew from about 300 billion in 1960 (earliest data available) to over $21 trillion in 2022 – a 70-fold increase. Figure

2.10 (US Department of Labor, Bureau of Labor Statistics 2023a) shows that the dollar has lost over half its purchasing power in the last 30 years. Since formation of the bank in 1913, it has lost 97 percent of its value.

Figure 2.9 M3 money supply since 1960

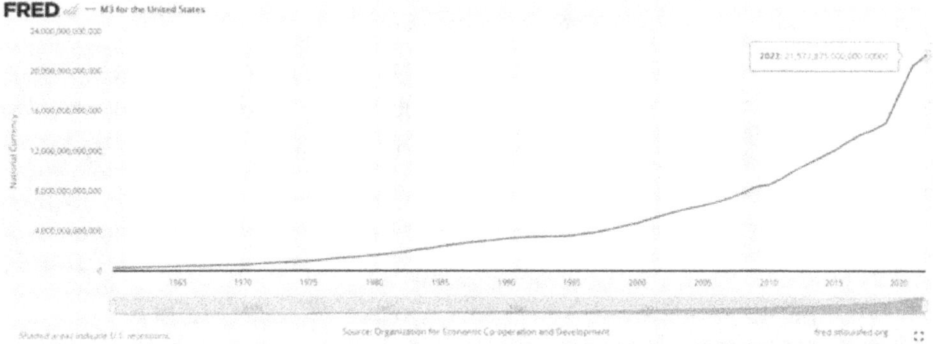

Figure 2.10 Dollar purchasing power since 1913

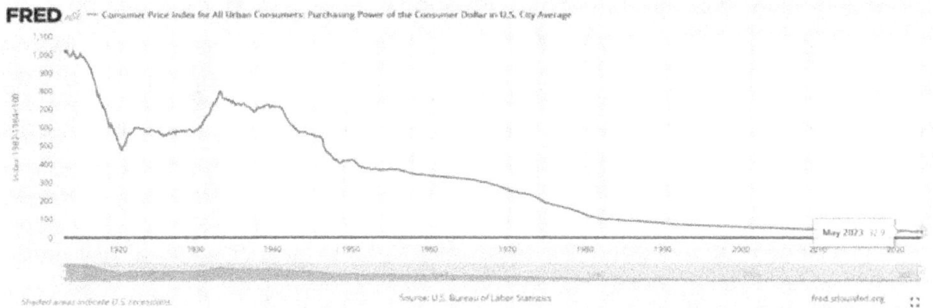

Stagnant wages would not be so problematic for workers if consumer prices were not rising. For this, we can thank steadfast determination by the US Treasury and the Federal Reserve Banks to maintain positive inflation of consumer prices. Absent their active collusion, market forces would have produced lower prices for most goods over the last thirty years. Why do the monetary czars fear deflation? Because it would upset the order they have established to ease borrowing by the government, prop up the banking system, and increase tax revenue. Inflation favors debtors by reducing the real value of loan repayments, which makes deficit spending – public or private – manageable and therefore good for creditors, as well. It also protects the income tax stake in avoiding any nominal reduction in wages. Mild inflation cannot continue indefinitely. Persistent underlying deflation thwarts the Fed's efforts to achieve its targeted inflation rate of two percent and damages its credibility. Even if they eventually succeed in suppressing deflation, the resulting inflation may not be controllable, which would also reduce confidence in the monetary system – its entire foundation (Rickards 2014: 258-60, 291).

Inflation of basic consumer goods prices imposes hardship, but its effects are especially harmful when it disproportionately impacts items like housing, education, and health care – all major household budget components that impact quality of life and opportunity. I'm afraid we've hit the trifecta, folks.

House prices have more than tripled over the last 30 years (US Federal Housing Finance Agency 2023). The affordable housing "crisis" that has stricken many US cities is a result of inflated real estate prices, courtesy of loose monetary policy. Many large and growing cities have experienced gentrification – new and richer residents replacing poorer residents. One of the most popular defense mechanisms, rent control, is ineffective. Alternatives usually involve other restrictions on growth or additional public spending to house people who can no longer afford to live in the city (Dougherty 2018). Thus, federal monetary policies that inherently favor wealthy individuals force local governments into policies that make it even more difficult to attract and retain residents. Tax policy is another factor – specifically, the mortgage interest deduction, which lowers after tax monthly payments for homeowners and encourages borrowing that bids up home sale prices. Eliminating this deduction would reduce demand for housing, especially in more expensive urban areas, that is driving prices higher for everyone when only those with six figure incomes can afford to buy.

The cost of higher education, as measured by the Higher Education Price Index, rose by 130 percent from 1991 to 2020 while the Consumer Price Index (CPI) rose 90 percent (US Department of Education 2020). This means that over the last 30 years, college costs rose 44 percent more than the overall cost of living – a troubling development when we consider that a degree is essential to enter or stay in the middle class. Rising costs have already led to the student loan crisis and are putting postsecondary education out of reach for lower income citizens. Another troublesome development in the US labor market is skyrocketing student debt and delinquency rates. In heated competition to join the ranks of college graduates who, as noted above, capture the best jobs available, students are paying whatever it takes to get a degree. We're not quite there yet, but education is looking more and more like sports; too many young people are sacrificing too much for a long shot at success.

"The improved economy has yet to mean higher wages for graduates already struggling to pay down massive debt, let alone ease the minds of students staring down the barrel of six-digit loan obligations yet to come." Student loan 90-day delinquency rates are over 10 percent – higher than those for credit card, auto loans, and mortgages. Continued increases in tuition and interest rates will make it even more difficult for graduates to make payments (Griffin 2018). What we're observing is not a college degree premium but a no-college-degree penalty – a consequence of supply and demand. Degree requirements no longer reflect actual needs; they exclude those unable to afford one. And failure to graduate can actually reduce lifetime earnings. We are not helping young people when we encourage unrealistic expectations that are often accompanied by crippling debt (Shell 2018: 152-7).

Over the last 30 years, per capita total national health care expenditures in the US rose by about $7500 in 2021 dollars (Telesford et al. 2023). As indicated in Figure 2.7, over the same period, the median US household income increased by just $12,000. This trend is clearly not sustainable. We waste a lot of money by making employer-paid health insurance premiums exempt from income tax. Employers have very little leverage because spending decisions are made by employees who typically pay a small fraction of the cost.[11] Providers have leverage over patients and plenty of incentive to encourage consumption of health care services. If employer-paid premiums were taxable to employees (still deductible to employers, like wages), more employees would demand and choose high deductible plans to reduce premiums, and these individuals and families would reduce consumption of health care services to limit their out-of-pocket expenses. This could significantly reduce national health care spending. The downside is that as consumers shoulder more responsibility for cost, some will forego preventive care. In any event, response to such a change by all parties is an iterative process that will take many years.

In this day and age, no one seems to question the assumption that an economy that is not growing by measures of aggregate spending such as Gross Domestic Product (GDP) is not healthy. It is true that low growth and recessions bring trouble, but that's because we've institutionalized the assumption to make it a self-fulfilling prophecy. Those who stand to gain from increases in the supply of money have managed to make it the law of the land. Metrics like GDP are inflated even with flatlined production, creating the illusion of real growth. If it falters, the Fed (presumably to stimulate full employment) has an excuse to print more money until it reaches its arbitrary 2 percent annual price inflation target. Having financialized the economy and hooked all the financial institutions on monetary heroin, the bank finds

---

[11] "On average, covered workers contribute 17% of the premium for single coverage and 28% of the premium for family coverage" (Claxton, et al 2022: 8). Out-of-pocket expenditures for health care are barely over 10 percent of the national total (Telesford et al. 2023).

it increasingly difficult to stop the spending that grows inequality, mostly, because of the Cantillon effect (Rouanet 2017).[12]

Overexpansion of the financial sector in the last several decades has misallocated capital, created booms and busts in the markets, and deterred real economic growth. It is ironic and tragic that capitalists insist on interventions in money markets even as they claim to support free markets in goods and services. Wall Street, which once upon a time actually helped direct savings toward their best use, has become a casino that uses other people's money to transfer wealth between traders. This ruins our economy by shifting financial and human resources from productive businesses to inflate assets such as stocks and real estate. "It can hardly be a coincidence that we've already had three unsustainable stock market bubbles since inequality began its upward march, one in each decade, with a fourth one just over the horizon. The long-term increase in the ratio of share prices to expected profits, the explosive growth in split-second computerized trading, the tidal wave of share buybacks, the fantastic sums being paid for new public companies – all of these are signs of too much capital chasing too few good investment opportunities" (Pearlstein 2018: 151-4).

Stock market indices no longer correlate with the health of the real economy. Enormous quantities of easy money and bailouts have inflated the value of all asset types, spawned new ones (e.g., nonfungible tokens), and led the cult of traders to believe "markets will never correct because the central bank just won't allow it." Flooding the system has led to a dangerous situation in which all assets rise and fall together, meaning there is no longer a safe haven (Stockman 2022: 142-3).

Rational choice, a highly influential economic theory, includes an assumption that people generally prefer more to less of any normal good or service, all other things being equal. However, 19th century sociologist Emile Durkheim (1984: 208-17, 276-82) claimed otherwise. Specialization and the enhanced productivity that emerges, he said, is a response to competitive pressure, not internal motivations. Population growth pushes us to the limits of what any given resource or skill can sustain, and we have no choice but to find other ways of being useful to society. Advance of civilization is an adaptation, not pursuit of dreams; moreover, seeking higher levels of activity than needed should be regarded as a societal disease.

In other words, we're addicted to economic growth. Obsessive overproduction leads to the false diagnosis of insufficient demand that prompts Keynesian stimulus

---

[12] Early 18th century economist Richard Cantillon explained that money creation favors those who first receive the newly created money because their incomes rise immediately, whereas others may only see their purchasing power decline as consumer price inflation comes about.

as a remedy. Demand is not insufficient when supply is an artifice of loose monetary policies, nor is it insufficient when prices are inflexible. Another way of looking at this is to recognize that supply side policies get the ball rolling and require even more stimulus on the demand side if we are to avoid disinflation. Evidence of this view is provided by a systems analysis of US economy dynamics. Bar-Yam et al. (2018: 38-40) conclude that excess borrowing since 1980 resulted in an oversupply of goods relative to demand for consumption. To correct this imbalance, they recommend monetary and fiscal policies that stimulate wages and consumption (vs. investment and capital). This is consistent with bottom-up proposals like UBI that arrive at the same solution for treating symptoms observed in macroeconomic data.

Today's one-two punch of monetary and fiscal policies that favor capital turn Say's law upside down by creating debt to produce things, then creating even more debt to buy those things. Jean-Baptiste Say was an early 19th century economist who postulated that supply creates its own demand. This is the basis of trade; production (that is not consumed) is the means of obtaining something else. We are reaping the whirlwind of pretending that modern economies work differently – a global deflationary recession in which we cannot service the debt needed to maintain consumption, never mind increase it to match government growth targets. David Stockman (2016: 47) puts it this way: "Under conditions of Peak Debt, therefore, the Keynesian credit magic ceases to 'stimulate' the Main Street economy. Instead, it never leaves the canyons of Wall Street, where it cycles in an incendiary spiral of leveraged speculation and the systematic inflation of financial assets." As evidence, he presents a comparison of the Wilshire 5000 stock market index with real median household income. From 1999 to 2014, the index rose by 125 percent while household income fell 7 percent.

In another book, Stockman (2013) explains in great detail that US monetary policy is rotten to the core, and has been since the Great Depression. The recent Troubled Asset Relief Program (TARP), Quantitative Easing (QE), and Tax Cuts and Jobs Act (TCJA) debacles were desperate attempts to prolong organized pillage of America's workers. In each case, our rich and powerful countrymen united behind the boldest of lies to justify policies that would save their skins at our expense. The engine for this corruption is the banking system's power to create money. Since money is essential to virtually every transaction in our economy, this is an enormous advantage (Rickards 2014: 69). Through the Federal Reserve System, bankers determine the quantity of money and its cost (interest rate). It also means that because the Fed controls the value of our currency, it controls the value of our labor. It should come as no surprise that their biggest customers – people who have lots of money – call the shots on lending practices. That's how we wound up with Too Big to Fail policies.

The bottom line is that money creation benefits the rich at others' expense. New money is inflationary; it dilutes the value of existing earnings and wealth through the law of supply and demand and (due to the Cantillon effect mentioned earlier) presents a supersized example of concentrated benefits and dispersed costs (Olson 1971). What is commonly referred to as inflation – the rate of price increases – is a function of not just monetary policy but interaction of many forces in the economy – especially productivity. If supply and demand for goods and services remain constant, an increase in the money supply would produce higher prices, because money would be relatively plentiful. However, technological progress enables production of more goods and services with the same inputs, offsetting the otherwise inflationary impact of an increase in the money supply. With a constant money supply, an increase in productivity would reduce prices. This would benefit consumers, yet it has been all but outlawed by the Fed's commitment to inflation targets (2 percent currently). Workers get to pay more for basic needs so bankers and their cronies have access to cheap credit and capture the benefits of any reduction in unit costs.

The vast majority of Americans have not just been poorly served by the Fed; we've been prostituted. Survival in this economy means, for most people, working for wages that are gradually but certainly confiscated by inflation. As David Stockman 2019: 231, 252) explains, pro-inflation policies "have functioned as a destroyer of competitiveness, good jobs, and real production-based wealth in the US economy…. As hundreds of millions of new low-cost industrial workers were recruited from the rice paddies of China and east Asia, the natural tendency was for domestic US wages and prices to deflate in order to preserve international competitiveness. But the Maestro [Alan Greenspan] and his money printers were having nothing to do with sound economics – electing instead to counteract the natural deflationary forces at loose in the world with massive expansion of domestic credit designed to keep domestic wages and prices continuously rising." It backfired, of course, because in real terms we got inflation of prices but not wages. Twenty years later, after watching Washington "perpetuate a monetary regime that swaps American labor and living standard in Flyover America for massively inflated financial asset prices on Wall Street," it's no wonder "the people out there in Rust Belt America… put a madman in the Oval Office to attack a system that truly is 'rigged' against them."

Other experts agree that rescues of financial institutions orchestrated by our central bank over the last 15 years were reckless. In 2010, former president of the Kansas City Federal Reserve Bank Thomas Hoenig tried stopping Quantitative

Easing (QE) because he knew it "would benefit a very small group of people who owned assets, and it would punish the very large group of people who lived on paychecks and tried to save money." Unfortunately, the Federal Open Market Committee (FOMC) was fond of consensus decision making (which some call groupthink), and his frequent dissents irritated other members. They did not share his concern about "allocative effects" of QE, so he pointed out how the easy money would increase risks in the economy as cash seeks higher yields. The final straw was his observation that this would just continue policies that led to the Great Financial Crisis of 2008. While several other regional bank presidents opposed QE for similar reasons, he was the only one with a vote, so the measure passed the FOMC 11-1. He retired in 2011 and continued writing and speaking about monetary policy in the hope that people outside the central bank headquarters would appreciate his informed opinions about the folly of short-term thinking (Leonard 2022: 9-21, 30-4, 301-3).

Somehow, most Americans buy the propaganda that the Federal Reserve Bank (Fed) exists to promote our interests, despite the obvious conflict of interest in its management by a board of bankers who have, according to insider Danielle DiMartino Booth (2017: 8, 251, 263-5) "become the fourth branch of the U.S. government." She documents how our central bank is run by academics whose economic models and decision making hardly consider the disastrous impact of their policies on regular people. Reforming the bank, she says, should begin with an act of Congress to release it from the dual mandate to control inflation and maximize employment. The bank should focus on price stability and leave employment to fiscal policy. The bank should also quit manipulative announcements regarding inflation expectations. Third, it should protect savings by setting a floor of 2 percent on overnight lending rates. Fourth, recruit business professionals (not academics) who have some knowledge of the real economy. Term limits, more voting power for district banks, cutting worthless research, equal opportunity hiring, and a commitment to letting the market work are a few of her additional recommendations.

Financial consultant Karen Petrou (2021: xviii-xxi) identifies the Fed as the "engine of inequality" that has been overlooked in most discussions of the chasm separating haves from have-nots in America. She cites many of the same indicators I have presented here as evidence that monetary policy is exacerbating the problem, and proposes a number of policy changes to "slow the engine and recalibrate its direction toward renewed economic equality." The first is to (as Booth recommended) return interest rates to a level that protects the savings of families – deliberately retracting the safety net they have placed under financial markets with ultra-low interest rates. Secondly, she would focus any future emergency support on families instead of corporations, i.e., ground-up vs. trickle-down. Third, she recommends Equality Banks to address allocation of affordable credit. And finally, she says, the Fed should take the lead on digital money, with legislative controls to enhance equal access and secure transactions.

I am pleased that these experts on banking agree the Fed lost its way, and I enthusiastically support their ideas to get it back on track. However, as a heterodox economist, I agree with Ron Paul (2009: 203) that we should abandon fiat money as soon as possible. "In an ideal world, the Fed would be abolished forthwith and the money stock frozen in place. That doesn't mean that there would be no more credit; rather, credit would be rooted in money saved, not money created." A stable money supply would restore the link between savings and investment that has been severed by the central bank. Those wishing to borrow would have to bargain with those who have savings by offering interest rates determined in a free market.

Without the power to create money, banks would have to be far more careful with investments and loan portfolios. This could devastate Wall Street and cause painful adjustments for many other businesses that have become dependent on easy money. On the other hand, sound money would provide long overdue relief to Main Street. Finally, the bounty of globalization and technological progress would flow to workers and consumers as inflation is held in check by a free market in money. Ending the Fed's monopoly would present opportunities for alternatives such as gold-backed dollars, Special Drawing Rights, and cryptocurrencies that may prove more responsive to market forces and appreciate or at least hold their value over time. Federal regulation would focus on safeguarding deposits and preventing fraudulent activity such as counterfeiting. We've had plenty of regulation, but for many decades it has been operating under rules written by the regulated (banking) community. It's about time our financial institutions actually help people achieve financial security. That cannot happen with the fox in charge of the hen house.

To be clear, I'm not suggesting we toss out the Fed just to replace it with another bank. That may or may not improve our system. I am calling for an end to the monopoly power. I've raised the issue because of its effects on income inequality, but these systems do far more damage. They destroy the primary function of markets – price discovery. "It is both ironic and tragic that Western central banks have embraced central planning with gusto in the early twenty-first century, not long after the Soviet Union and Communist China abandoned it in the late twentieth…. The central planner must suspend belief in one's own intervention to gather information about the intervention's effects. But that information is a false signal because it is not the result of a free-market activity. This is a recursive function…. The more these institutions intervene in markets, the less they know about real economic conditions, and the greater the need to intervene" (Rickards 2014: 69, 87). The most ardent supporters of intervention in money markets are so-called capitalists who espouse belief in free markets while relying on artificially low interest rates to fund their financial shenanigans. It's time for another kind of intervention – resignation of the chief enabler to their addiction. If we can transition to a free market for money, inflation will abate, prices will reflect real market demand and supply, and our financial system will no longer pose a mortal threat to the global economy.

Most Americans are deeply in debt of some kind. Most have a positive net worth, i.e., the value of their assets exceeds their obligations. But even those with significant means have very little liquidity; they live from one paycheck to the next. This is disturbing, especially considering we are the richest nation in a highly advanced economic system – and we had better pay attention because it's happened in a period of tremendous growth. "In the 1950s and '60s, American economic growth democratized prosperity. In the 2010s, we have managed to democratize financial insecurity." Economists have noted the irony that increased credit, which is supposed to improve financial security, has contributed instead to distress. Some blame the financially illiterate victims (Gabler 2016). I blame those who should know better – the geniuses at the Fed who have delivered negative real interest rates and politicians who demand monetization of debt created by their fiscal policies.

The central bank and our elected officials may or may not understand what their policy choices are doing to average Americans, but they undoubtedly understand what pleases Wall Street. Stock markets benefit from cheap leverage and less competition from bonds with low yields. Those with access to capital prosper while the working class settles for virtually zero interest on their savings accounts. Older workers are being forced to feed the stock market casino, because they cannot work long enough or save enough of their wages to provide a decent retirement income without taking more risk than they might like. In a free market for money, bankers would be the ones at risk. They would not be able to control their cost of supply through Fed policy; rather, they would have to borrow at interest rates consistent with loan demand that fully compensates savers for their risk and inconvenience. Asset prices would reflect use value instead of artificially inflated collateral value (sources of funds for speculation). Debt would fund investment instead of consumption.

We the People have been negligent in our duty to "secure the Blessings of Liberty to ourselves and our Posterity" (US Constitution 1787). I deplore the argument that national debt is money "we" owe ourselves. First of all, the we who spend is not the we who pay, even in the short term. That may be justifiable if spending and taxation policies reflect a fair and open democratic process. It's another story entirely if those who pay aren't eligible to vote or aren't even alive. "We" who authorize spending the money can all conveniently agree upon "investments" that will create jobs and profits today and may benefit future generations. But good intentions don't secure the blessings of liberty; tomorrow's workers will pay directly (by taxation) or indirectly (through inflation) and find their fiscal options limited, thanks to our profligacy.

We commonly think of taxes as payment for services, and most of us do not quibble about whether we have real choice in the matter or whether we're getting value. The thing is, taxes have not always emerged as solutions to public problems, such as how to provide roads and schools. Sometimes the taxes are imposed to fund rulers' ambitions. As David Graeber (2014: 49-51, 364-8) says in explaining the state theory of money, "Governments demand taxes because they wish to get their hands on people's money." Markets did not emerge spontaneously to replace barter and then lead to creation of money; rather, rulers created money to facilitate taxation, and they needed markets to provision their armies. People were taught to work for wages so they could pay taxes. They were also taught to consume goods they did not necessarily need. This is not a relic; we have institutionalized the marriage of warriors and financiers through central banking. Virtually all of our debt is due to military expenditures, which in turn enforce the dollar's reserve currency status. Others continue to accept our currency as a debt they know will never be repaid – effectively a global tax that supports our imperial projection of military power.

While it's common knowledge that Congress no longer pretends to worry about balancing budgets, there seems to be very little understanding that all federal spending is facilitated by deliberate depreciation of the dollar. We're not only passing on debt to future generations; we're bequeathing a currency that is losing its foundation – trust. Monetary and fiscal policies present a classic chicken/egg dilemma. Given the free money option, of course we are going to borrow; we spend more because we can. At the same time, the pressure to spend more and tax less is overwhelming and relentless. We're so spoiled by deficit spending that we now face a serious challenge in convincing voters that we can pay our own way. SSBI, by weaning us off the Ponzi retirement scheme, is a significant step toward balancing the budget. It will whittle away at the (huge) obligations, but just as importantly, it will end mandatory classification of entitlement spending – a practice that places all budget projections deep enough in deficit territory to provide cover for hundreds of billions of dollars in discretionary shenanigans.

In FY 2022, servicing our enormous debt cost $724 billion dollars (Statista 2023), which is comparable to total defense ($751 billion) and nondefense ($910 billion) outlays (US CBO 2023a). The burden is sure to grow as interest rates rise. US spending deficits are so large that they would not be possible without intervention by the Fed to keep interest rates low. The mainstream view is that this is an advantage of central banking. But who actually benefits from deficit spending? The one percent, of course. The rest of us share the debt that was created to benefit special interests. Politicians like to blame the deficit on entitlements like Social Security and Medicare benefits that they have designated mandatory (meaning not subject to annual appropriations). These are fairly predictable expenses – and yet Congress manages to routinely produce deficits that exceed the total level (~$1 trillion) of annual discretionary spending. If spending were limited to revenues and prioritized general interests, what would stay and what would go? Voters would choose to fully fund core services provided by direct federal programs (like the mandatory entitlements) and forgo discretionary programs that benefit organizations with powerful lobbies. Putting discretionary spending on the national credit card avoids the politically suicidal tax question entirely.

Monetization of the debt devalues the currency and thereby harms many (especially poor) consumers who would not have paid the taxes needed for a balanced budget. As noted by Thomas Piketty (2017: 700), "From the standpoint of the general interest, it is normally preferable to tax the wealthy rather than borrow from them." It is telling that for the last 40 years, people sworn to protect our interests have consistently chosen to borrow. Some dismiss concerns about deficits with a rationalization that we owe it to ourselves or with an argument that lower taxation produces higher tax revenue.[13] Both are nonsense. Public debt is created by those who get to spend the money and thereby benefit directly; in one form or another future spending is thereby reduced and this cost is distributed among an entirely different set of individuals.

By far the largest form of federal welfare to big business is cheap credit. The Fed is purportedly independent and driven by commitments to price stability and full employment. But because it is controlled by bankers, it is committed first and foremost to banking, and its primary tool – a monopoly on the money supply – is used to maintain member banks' competitive edge by keeping interest rates as low as possible. Cheap debt has led to asset inflation – which clearly favors the rich (Piketty 2017: 574-8, Standing 2016: 120-6). Over the last 25 years, real wages have fallen to

---

[13] The tax idea is illustrated by the Laffer curve, which was created by Arthur Laffer and used to justify President Reagan's tax cuts in the 1980s. Laffer plotted tax rates on the x axis and revenue on the y axis, predicting an inverted U shape that peaked at a moderate level of taxation because higher rates disincentivize production.

such an extent that the middle class is shrinking, with many Americans dangerously in debt. And the labor force participation rate is so low that the official unemployment rate is meaningless. In other words, the Fed has aided and abetted upward redistribution of wealth.[14]

Capitalists do not value work; they value profit, which in today's economy does not require investment in production of goods and services for consumers. The banks, which thanks to repeal of Glass-Steagall[15] can use the money for just about anything, have vastly expanded use of financial instruments. Purely financial transactions are more liquid and less transparent – meaning profits or losses can be taken quickly and without all the muss and fuss of businesses that serve consumers (and require human labor). The Fed's (low interest rate) subsidy of debt-driven financial speculation has simultaneously increased the price of assets and reduced demand for labor (hence wages). No wonder the middle class is struggling.

Clearly, all is not well in the land of the free and the home of the brave. The fortunate few are living the dream while the unfortunate many are wondering what to do with theirs. Sound money could be the single most effective weapon for fighting income inequality in the long run. But change of that magnitude is even more ambitious than SSBI, politically. As we consider and work toward monetary changes, we should pursue fiscal policies that neutralize the pernicious effects of inflation. SSBI is a counterweight that disperses some of those benefits to offset the costs of corruption and poor policy decisions to the masses.

SSBI is unconditional; it focuses on helping the poor, no matter who they are. It replaces existing (targeted) transfers to more efficiently distribute tax dollars and to protect beneficiaries from intrusive requirements. SSBI avoids the poverty trap created by programs that reduce or deny benefits to the working poor. Funding Social Security and Medicare benefits with income taxes instead of a payroll tax removes a disincentive for employers to hire or retain an individual (15.3 percent tax on their labor) and encourages workers to enter or stay in the labor force. It also shifts the burden from the working poor to higher income households. Those who never escape poverty will continue to receive help, but those whose incomes rise will join the net contributors. SSBI thus becomes not just a solution to income inequality and debt financing of social welfare of all kinds; it is a unifying force.

---

[14] Fiscal policy contributes to inequality, as well. For example, Marr and Highsmith (2012: 9) note that depreciation of equipment financing by corporations in addition to the interest paid amounts to a 46 percent subsidy! To put this in perspective, the U.S. tax code favors debt over equity financing by a greater margin (70%) than any other industrialized country.
[15] This 1933 Act, which separated commercial from investment banking, was repealed in 1999.

Chapter 3. Nothing to Lose but Shackles

The data presented in Chapter 2 have been in plain sight for a decade, and hardly a day passes without another scholar or journalist offering analysis and policy recommendations on the future of work. Of course, most of them stay within the boundaries of existing institutions. Criticizing the Tax Cuts and Jobs Act of 2017 (TCJA) and other forms of corporate welfare, calling for more progressive taxation, endorsing increases to the minimum wage, and demanding improved access or higher funding levels for public assistance programs are all examples of solutions that implicitly accept the rules of a game that is rigged against the average American. But playing by those rules will continue the current trend, regardless of how skillfully and passionately we fight to win. The world has changed so much – and in such a way as to aggravate the problems – that we need to be far more creative.

Rules that in my opinion have limited our vision and policy options include:

1. American citizens (We the People) need government to "grow the economy."
2. We need government to make us save money and to keep it for us.
3. We need government to create jobs and to make us work.
4. We need government to make us go to school.
5. We need government to create money.

I'm not saying we do not need government. I'm also not saying we should immediately jettison any and all policies that institutionalize and operationalize these rules. What I am saying is that if we are serious about solving the problems of poverty and income inequality, we must set our own minds free of the bias presented by failing to question the policies that got us where we are today. I've already hinted at a few of these ideas, will discuss most of them in this chapter, and I'll touch on all of them at some point in this book. Each might make an interesting essay, but these simple statements are more powerful just as they are. Please read them again and ask yourself if they describe what you want from your government.

This chapter explores questions about work-related policies and incentives such as taxation and income support to make the case for adopting a BIG in the US.

Tax Cuts and Jobs Act: Seriously?

Wall Street had a very good year in 2017; stock exchange indices set new highs and *then* (in December) Congress delivered and President Trump signed the TCJA – a present that had been on their wish list for years. Workers got another promise of trickle-down benefits that was not taken seriously.

The TCJA aimed to further increase investment, which was already very healthy, thanks to years of near zero interest rates courtesy of the Fed. Research indicated cutting corporate tax rates would do very little to boost employment or productivity and, since the top one percent of households accounted for 47 percent of the incidence of corporate income tax, such cuts would boost incomes substantially more for richer households. It's not as if corporations had been carrying a heavy load to begin with. Effective US tax rates were in line with those of other advanced economies. Corporate tax revenues fell from 5.9 percent of GDP in 1952 to 1.9 percent in 2015, despite historically large profits in recent years, due to the success of US corporations in exploiting tax loopholes (Bivens and Blair 2017: 2-3). Moreover, as indicated in Figure 3.1 (Tax Policy Center 2022), this reduced burden came at workers' expense because payroll tax revenues rose by a similar percent of GDP over the same period.

Figure 3.1 Payroll taxes replace corporate income taxes

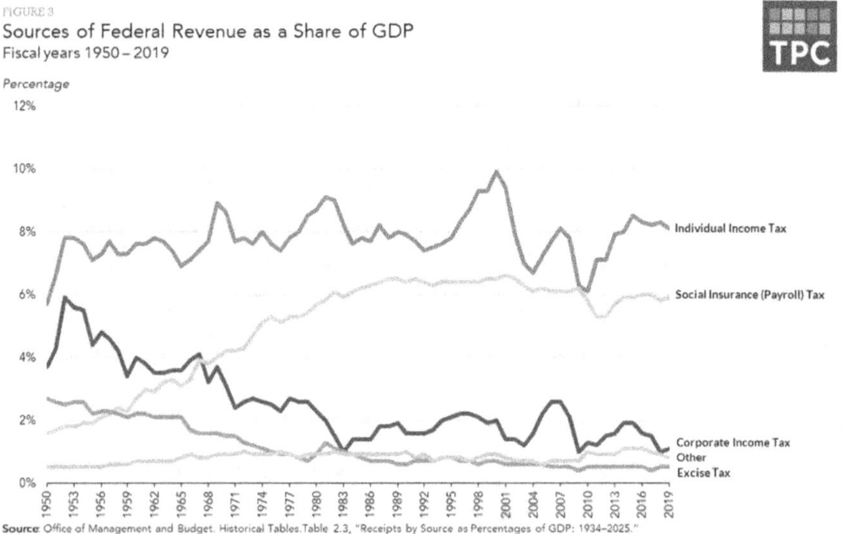

We do have a jobs problem that has been caused by policies that favor investment in capital at the expense of labor – especially policies that encourage debt. "The U.S. tax code favors capital investment, offering low marginal rates on capital income, rapid rates of depreciation on plant and equipment investments, and, in many cases, directly subsidizing capital expenditure (e.g., the R&D tax credit). Similar subsidies for investments in labor and skills are lacking. As a result, the effective tax rate on human capital investments – in the form of labor income taxes – greatly exceeds the tax rate on capital investments. This imbalance between the taxation of human versus physical capital investments gives firms an incentive to replace workers with tax-subsidized machinery where possible; indeed, one reason that firms may adopt 'so-so' technologies is because taxpayers implicitly subsidize labor-replacing capital investments" (Autor, Mindell, and Reynolds 2019: 41). More of the same only makes this problem worse.

A Brookings Institution study conducted several years after the new tax law went into effect found that its supply-side incentives had little effect on investment or wages, and repatriated funds were largely used to finance stock repurchases. "The Trump administration claimed that the TCJA would provide significant benefits to workers… [and] the Council of Economic Advisors …predicted that annual *median* household wages would rise by $3,000 to 7,000… There is no evidence that any wage response close to these claims occurred in 2018 and 2019… The patterns in the data suggest instead that corporate tax cuts did not help workers very much" (Gale and Haldeman 2021, italics original). In a 2019 National Association for Business Economics survey cited by the Brookings study, "84 percent of businesses reported that the tax cut had not altered their investment or hiring decisions."

If we want more jobs, we ought to look at policies that are directly tied to hiring. A plan designed to benefit most US citizens would be supported by analysis of the record low labor force participation rate and stagnant wages. It would ask and answer questions like "How can we make it easier for businesses to hire workers and for workers to support their families?" Real reform focused on jobs, fairness, and better wages would take a very different approach. Eliminating the payroll tax, for example, would reduce the cost of hiring and increase compensation for every employer and worker. For many if not most wage earners, it is a larger burden than the federal income tax. Moreover, the payroll tax "makes middle-class labor the most highly taxed factor of production in the entire economy" (Markovits 2019: 281). It seizes the first 15.3 percent of earnings *from every small business owner* to fund Social Security and Medicare. This extremely regressive tax kills small businesses. Anyone who has ever started a business knows that cash is dearest in the early years. "Saving" for retirement should be deferred until the enterprise generates positive cash flow. It's a real slap in the face to entrepreneurs that our federal government justifies bailouts of big business to save jobs yet keeps the ball-and-chain payroll tax firmly in place.

We should pay more attention to marginal tax rates faced by low- and moderate-income workers. Federal income taxes are low for this group, but Figure 3.2 indicates when we include payroll taxes, state income taxes, and food stamp benefits, we find that those with low incomes often keep less of additional earnings than those with high incomes (US CBO 2012: vii). Doesn't this discourage work?

Figure 3.2 Marginal tax rates highest for lowest incomes

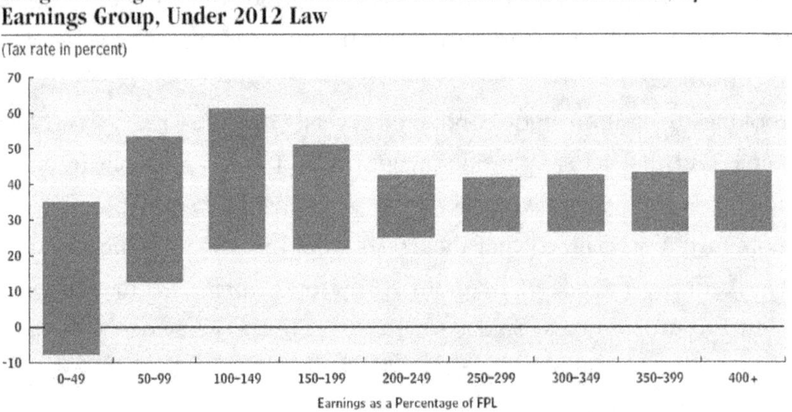

Source: Congressional Budget Office based on a public-use sample of tax returns from the Internal Revenue Service and survey data from the Census Bureau.

Notes: CBO's simulations of tax liabilities and SNAP benefits were based on information from a public-use sample of income tax returns filed in 2006 supplemented with information from the 2007 Annual Social and Economic Supplement of the Current Population Survey and the 2006 American Community Survey. The sample was restricted to taxpayers under the age of 65 who were not disabled, who had earnings in 2006, and whose adjusted gross income was below 450 percent of federal poverty guidelines. It was weighted to be representative of the population of tax filers.

The simulated marginal tax rates include the combined effects of federal individual income taxes, state individual income taxes (under provisions in effect in 2006), federal payroll taxes, and the reduction in SNAP benefits. The simulated marginal tax rates were based on taxpayers' total compensation before their employers' share of payroll taxes was deducted.

FPL = federal poverty guidelines; SNAP = Supplemental Nutrition Assistance Program (formerly known as the Food Stamp program).

Generally, when any government – state, local, or federal – makes its case for spending or tax breaks on the jobs that will be created (which is just about all the time), we should apply the rule that if it sounds too good to be true, it usually is. Of course, there will be new jobs, but at whose expense? Interest in growth and jobs is a given for politicians; however, we should challenge their use of the term "job creator" at every turn, because it so clearly and inappropriately assumes employers are benevolent agents of the government. Existence of a job is just as dependent on a person's willingness to work as it is on an employer's willingness to pay. Yet large businesses (e.g., Amazon, which famously solicited bids for its new headquarters in 2018) have come to expect tax concessions and far too often, elected officials take the bait. The agreement may include guarantees of employment and even wages, but gains for the newcomers are offset by losses to some of the businesses and workers who have invested in the community for years without subsidies. Some of them will be priced out of property and labor markets. There is no such thing as a free lunch (Slattery and Zidar 2020).

Just to be clear: I'm not saying growth is bad or taxes are good. I just argued that we should reduce payroll taxes so people can start and grow small businesses. I'm saying it's wrong and unproductive for society when government plays favorites in the market. Intervention should be neutral; the same rule should apply to everyone. I am just as strongly opposed to protectionism. A business that decides to relocate without bribing or being bribed deserves fair treatment. Existing businesses and workers should not expect immunity to competition. That would be unfair to residents who may benefit from increasing property values, demand for services, and higher wages. Opening the door to exemptions creates a market for exemptions – a Pandora's box of rent-seeking – that is like catnip to politicians and the corporations, wealthy individuals, and special interests they rely on to gain or retain office.

Work is Different These Days

For most of the 20th century, we had a competitive market for labor, but things are different now. Wages are stagnant, benefits are not as generous, and fewer jobs are full-time and permanent in this "gig" economy. Poor Americans face the daunting task of navigating the maze of public assistance programs and a labor market that offers cold comfort. Luke Shaefer (2016) refers to "precarious" working conditions of the poor such as scarce or nonexistent paid time off and overtime, work off the clock, just-in-time scheduling, and unhealthy workplaces. This is unfortunate, and our reluctance to adjust public policies has made the situation worse. We need to consider what can reasonably be expected of workers in this environment.

Technology has completely changed the nature of work, mostly to the good. Stories abound of people who enjoy flexibilities unheard of in the 20th century. Yet there is a dark side. The so-called gig economy has created a buyer's market for piecework labor that can be performed by anyone, anywhere. Desperate people who cannot find regular employment literally hunt for work posted on Mechanical Turk, Uber, and TaskRabbit that pays them (as independent contractors, i.e., not protected by minimum wage laws) an average of $4-5/hour. About 5 percent of Americans are doing this kind of work, and even more are expected to turn to it in the next decade (Semuels 2018).

Other examples of how technology and outsourcing have profited business owners at the expense of workers is Amazon's use of vendors whom it pays by the package and trucking companies' monitoring of drivers. Brishen Rogers (2017) notes that "some workers will thrive as their unique skills and talents are rewarded by new technologies, many others will have less autonomy, less generous wages, less time for social connection, and unpredictable schedules." With more contractual relationships and less formal employment and collective bargaining, workers will have less power to improve their wages and working conditions. A basic income helps solve poverty problems but may enable rather than counteract exploitation by employers. For this reason, Rogers recommends supplementing income support with labor law reforms.

Over the last decade, college graduates have captured "all" of the net new jobs created, while the number of employed Americans with a high school education or less has declined (Shapiro 2018). The financial crisis accounts for the loss; however, as job opportunities for those without a college degree did not reach pre-recession levels, millions of them became discouraged and left the labor force. Official statistics (low unemployment rates) suggest a healthy labor market; some are even crowing about "full employment." But numerous employers and workers are not happy. Businesses are not finding "qualified" workers, but the problem may be that they fail to offer sufficient wages and good working conditions (Lowrey 2018b). Low-paid service jobs are growing much faster than well-paid high-tech jobs.[16] The "good workers" employers claim cannot be found simply do not want the precarious jobs on offer. As Alpert et al. (2019: 12) put it, "[t]he problem in the U.S. employment situation is that the quality of the jobs that are on offer (as measured by relative weekly pay) has, by and large, been declining. And that fact is (a) one of the principal drivers of the sustained depression of the U.S. labor force participation rate and increase in the number of workers marginally attached to the labor force; and (b) a missing link in assessments of labor slack and job openings in the U.S."

Former World Bank chief economist Paul Romer says the US suffers from a "work disorder" that will require treatment by a change in the rules to create better jobs. Low pay is not the only problem here; workers' relationships, health, and self-esteem are casualties of a system that relies on cheap labor. We will not improve morale with continued beatings. Somehow, we need to flip this around so that instead of expecting workers to meet the demands of a job, workers are empowered to choose

---

[16] Automation (along with international trade) is displacing middle-skill workers. The resulting polarized labor market concentrates rewards among the highly skilled and educated workers while devaluing (presumably by increasing supply) non-specialized work (Autor, Mindell, and Reynolds 2019: 22).

work that actually provides meaning to life – the kind we refer to when we speak of a work ethic (Shell 2018: 60-7, 233-6).

As Oren Cass (2018: 102-3) explains, despite our best efforts to educate everyone, the fact is that not every student will succeed:

> Roughly speaking, one-fifth of all students were already off-track and did not join their classmates crossing the [high school diploma] stage. Another fifth will move from their senior year to something besides further schooling. The third fifth will enroll in college but fail to complete it. Yet another fifth will complete some form of college but land in jobs that don't require the degree they just earned. Despite decades of reform in teacher training, student testing, and standards, as well as school choice and hundreds of billions of dollars in new annual education spending, only a final fifth will successfully navigate the path – high school to college to career – that is our education system's ideal.

I agree with Cass' suggestion that we try a different approach. Instead of insisting that everyone try what works for just one fifth of us, let's do what every other developed country has done, which is to help students develop and market their demonstrated aptitudes. We have invested heavily in vocational training programs, but more as a remedy for adult unemployment than proactively preparing youth – and they have not proven to be good investments (Fortson et al. 2017).

Progressive BIG proponents think the freedom to redefine work is one of its major benefits. Experiments that illustrate how it liberates individuals to pursue their "labor of love" include a pilot in Ontario, Canada in which about 4000 people received stipends that lifted them to at least 75 percent of official poverty level incomes (Bergstein 2018). In one town where about 10 percent of the population received the stipend, there was a noticeable increase in retail business and citizens' attitudes. But more to the point, the stipend enabled individuals to keep low-paying jobs such as museum curator, do volunteer work, and finish college. People in the town were more engaged in productive endeavors (work) without necessarily having more "jobs." Others have pointed out that unconditional transfers to lower income households, which have a higher propensity to consume, increases output, employment, prices, and wages (Nikiforos, Steinbaum, and Zezza 2017).

As I pointed out in Chapter 1, we have a culture and institutions that equate jobs with income, and therein lies the problem. We all need income, yet not everyone can get a job. Well known basic income advocate Scott Santens (2018) presented data in Figure 3.3 on the nature of work that helps explain why college graduates are capturing new jobs at the expense of those with less education. This whole conversation is about adapting to the new economy, but his approach is to recognize that what is required is more fundamental because we made the mistake long ago of requiring work in exchange for food, water, and shelter. Now machines do most of the work, so we have a surplus of labor. This is why the labor force participation rate is low and median wages have not grown with the economy. Common policy responses are so lacking in understanding or imagination that they include even more work requirements for public assistance and job guarantees. Santens says, "[P]erhaps jobs have become the problem, not the solution," which is why basic income – by severing the knot tying income to work – is the way out of technological unemployment.

Figure 3.3 Work is changing

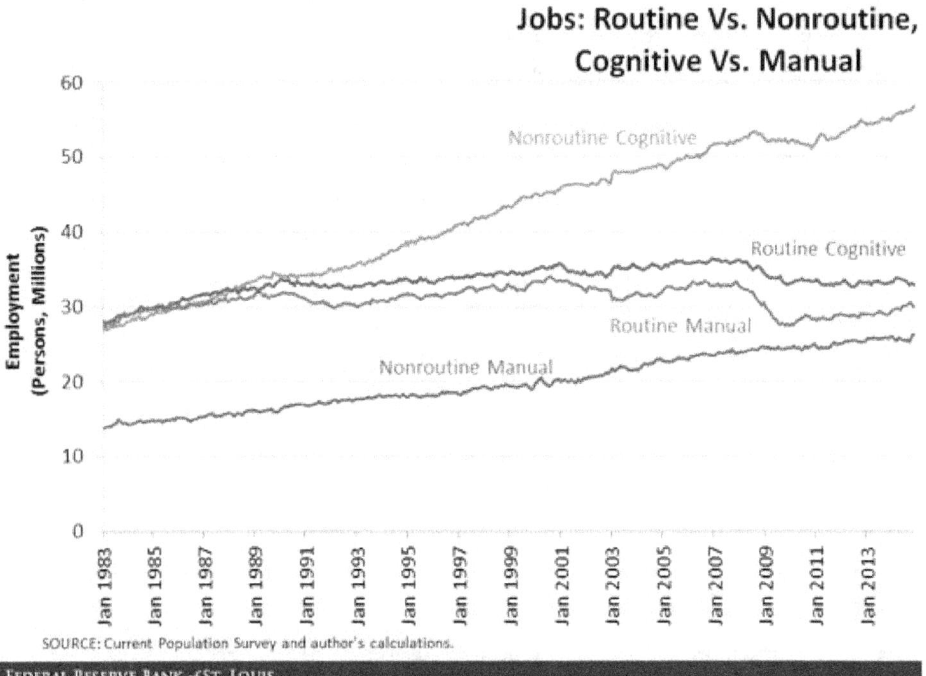

Santens has put his finger on the crux of the matter. As I indicated earlier, our work ethic has such a hold on our society that we find it extremely difficult to imagine unconditional assistance. That's easy to understand. What's troubling is that we don't seem capable of learning from mistakes. In the article introducing SSBI (Richardson 2013: 109), I referred to England's Poor Laws as a case in point. In their 19th century version of workfare, Irish workers were housed and fed in workhouses until the program expanded to include English workers whose wages were depressed by competition from the subsidized Irish, and the program became too expensive. The scheme failed because of the focus on jobs instead of poverty.

Yet another insight from Santens (2018) is that our attempts to employ everyone are actually hindering the progress available through automation because we're forcing people into less productive jobs and – because they're paid so little – making it less worthwhile to invest in technology that could make those jobs easier or unnecessary. Moreover, reduced discretionary incomes make machines' products less affordable to workers, limiting markets and sustainable growth. The beauty of UBI is that it creates a closed-loop ecosystem in which income circulates from top to bottom and back again (like water in our atmosphere, rivers, lakes, and oceans).

We Don't Need the Middlemen

Many of our problems can be traced to unnecessary and counterproductive growth of our federal government. Small government is no longer an option. That doesn't mean self-government cannot make a comeback. Self-government means asking less of others and more of ourselves. Since politicians have demonstrated they cannot be trusted with power, we should withdraw that power. In doing so, we should be far less concerned about which party controls the White House, the Senate, the House of Representatives, or the Supreme Court, and focus on the growing exploitation of the working class by the ruling class. US voters have allowed exploitation of workers by the "job creators" who have taken control of the federal work/welfare/tax system. It's time to try something different – redistributing the wealth and empowering all citizens to participate in a rapidly changing economy.

Fifty years ago, power in the labor market was more balanced; employers and workers shared the benefits of productivity growth. Since then, wages have not kept up, and yet the ruling class responds to the evidence with policies such as the recent corporate tax cut (Gould 2015). Voters who are fed up with this sort of representation need to insist on change but may not know where to begin. Most Americans have no choice but to work for others in pursuit of life, liberty, and happiness. We should put freedom first by enacting policies that provide citizens the widest possible choice regarding our own labor.

Most politicians seem to have no qualms about using tax breaks to attract or retain business (and their campaign contributions). One rationale to justify federal tax expenditures is that it merely allows taxpayers to keep their own money. This is a moral argument to distinguish corporate welfare from direct spending forms of welfare that benefit individuals and – in a fantasy world wherein revenues match expenditures – require taxing someone else. Either way, it's a spending decision, and debates properly center on whether the money is well spent. What's troubling, though, is that we have routinely applied a double standard. Tax expenditures are "neutral, invisible policies like the mortgage interest deduction" that benefit the wealthy, while benefit programs for the poor are means-tested. We trust people who can afford to purchase homes and make other (often spectacular) purchases to do so in ways that benefit society. Some of them take millions of dollars in deductions that only in theory are subject to audit. Yet we subject people who seek the stingiest of benefits to humiliating scrutiny and conditions. Not only do we think everyone should work, no matter what the pay or conditions. We don't trust poor people with money. Annie Lowrey (2018a: 117-8, 141, italics original) calls it our "Puritanical obsession with differentiating the deserving from the undeserving…. The issue is not that the United States cannot pull its people above the poverty line, but that it does not *want* to…. [M]eans testing allows the government to exclude many of the poor."

We have turned benefit payments and tax deductions into entitlements for those who fit our merit-based criteria. This reflects and reinforces divisions that help the ruling class maintain power and advantage. From targeted incentives to more widely distributed tax expenditures like employer-paid health insurance and the mortgage interest deduction, we provide benefits to the wealthy with no questions asked. Meanwhile, we subject applicants for public assistance to humiliating scrutiny. This has been effective in reducing direct public expense, which has been presented as evidence of success in welfare reform. A more honest appraisal would find such policies hypocritical and inhumane. Unconditional, universal benefits could stop this cycle of discrimination.[17]

The simple, obvious solution to poverty and inequality is to give directly to the poor, whose misery provides a laser focus on their immediate needs. A nonprofit organization named GiveDirectly has documented improvements in the lives of Kenyan villagers after committing generous monthly payments to each resident for twelve years. They offered poverty relief to people not by giving them goods and services donors thought they needed (with paternalistic strings attached), as so many other non-governmental organizations have done, but by assisting them with cash, unconditionally. This project, among others, is convincing aid providers of all kinds, including disaster relief charities, that cash is more efficient and ultimately more humane than donor-specified forms of assistance (Lowrey 2018a: Ch. 4).

Michael Tanner (2015: 7-8) favors an incremental approach to welfare reform but identifies several advantages to a guaranteed income approach, such as greater

---

[17] Race-based discrimination is implied because white Americans are much wealthier, on average, than black Americans. In any event, it's a wrong that is overdue for correction.

efficiency, reduced paternalism, better incentives (to work and to marry), and effective reduction of poverty. It would reduce rent-seeking by landlords, health care providers, farmers, and other special interests who benefit from having policy makers and bureaucrats making decisions for beneficiaries that they would make for themselves if they were given cash. Universal benefits also eliminate discrimination inherent in determinations of eligibility.

Entrepreneur and presidential candidate Andrew Yang (2018: 72-3) has published a book declaring that UBI is the answer to our jobs problem. He calls the establishment's tone-deaf insistence on flawed data and policies a "war on normal people" that must be ended by responsive leadership and an about face in public policies. For example, he challenges the mainstream assumption that the efficient market hypothesis can be applied to labor, especially today. Retraining has not been effective and it is even less promising now: "The problem is that the new jobs are almost certain to be in different places than existing ones and will be less numerous than the ones that disappear. They will generally require higher levels of education than the displaced workers have. And it will be very unlikely for a displaced worker to move, identify the need, gain skills, and fill the new role."[18]

David Graeber (2018: 261, italics original) also pointed to UBI as a preferred alternative to the status quo, in which millions of people waste their time and other resources performing "bullshit jobs." He, too, identifies numerous myths that guide policies, most of which are discussed in this book. Above all, though, he calls attention to the absurdity of our situation: "It's harder to imagine a surer sign that one is dealing with an irrational economic system than the fact that the prospect of eliminating drudgery is considered to be a *problem*."

Not everyone is convinced UBI would work. For example, Bob Greenstein (2017) argues that it would actually increase poverty because it would come at the expense of existing welfare programs. But he assumes Social Security and Medicare would remain untouched, that most of a UBI would be funded with additional taxes, and that it would be unpopular because it would be available to people who are unemployed but not elderly or disabled. Means-tested programs work, he says, because they have survived. This is the political equivalent of the efficient market hypothesis – a claim that if it was feasible, we would already have it and therefore it is not feasible. He's not alone. This illustrates the challenge we face in convincing Americans accustomed to many decades of payroll taxes and workfare programs that the time has come to try something else. Existing programs are working for many

---

[18] See also Frey 2019: 245-8.

people (especially those who authorize, fund, or administer them) and naturally, they have no incentive to support change. So, conservative critics such as Greenstein have a point that cannot be ignored; it's not enough to make a moral case for UBI. To achieve consensus, we need to tackle the fiscal challenges and show not only that it can be done but that the proposed redistribution of income will benefit the vast majority of Americans.

BIG critics express concern that it would decrease incentives to work. With record low participation in the labor force, it is reasonable to worry about making things worse. However, we should take a closer look at causes. If incentives were sufficient, we would be observing different statistics. In the US, we're particularly sensitive to socialism as an equalizing force that destroys incentives. Perhaps that fear has led us to destroy incentives by moving toward the other extreme – institutionalized transfers to the wealthy. American workers may not care whether their taxes benefit the poor or the wealthy, but the impact on their incomes, well-being, and incentives to work is the same either way. Steven Pearlstein (2018: 136-7) illustrated the macroeconomic effect by adapting the famous inverted u-shaped Laffer Curve to create what he calls the Pearlstein Curve, a graphic with output per person on the y axis and the level of (income) inequality on the x axis. Either extreme yields virtually zero output; the maximum lies somewhere near the middle.

More common objections to BIG are emotional; they may reflect a general dislike of work and resentment of others' getting by without it, combined with an inherited guilt trip notion that we have to earn the right to exist. Some even believe a poverty level BIG will be so attractive to people who are already working or fully capable of doing so that they will leave the labor market altogether, eager to use "our money" to indulge in selfish, destructive activities:

A job provides much more than a paycheck. At a basic level, work occupies our time, which can be quite good in and of itself. (Do you want to live in a world filled with young men who don't need to work?) Perhaps more significantly, working liberates us from our passions by directing them to the end of social improvement, creating a society characterized by mutual contribution, mutual dependence and mutual obligation. In a UBI world, those who choose to work will support those who choose not to — not those who can't work, but those who won't. This really would be a world of makers and takers (Strain 2016).

The author of this passage proudly admits it is paternalistic, but sadly, he is far from alone in his cynicism.[19] If work is so important that everyone should experience it, why not protect us from inheritance? Yet Congress doubled the estate tax exclusion to $12 million in the TCJA.

This double standard with regard to UBI – assuming others would make worse choices than we would make for ourselves – is also evident in survey data presented by recent Nobel laureates and behavioral economists Esther Duflo and Abhijit Banerjee (2019) indicating 49 percent of respondents thought "many people" would stop working if there were a $13,000 annual guaranteed income. However, only 12 percent of them said they would stop working themselves. As a reality check, the authors also present empirical data on the Alaska Permanent Fund, a mineral royalty trust. Since 1982, the state has paid annual dividends averaging about $5000 per household. Labor force participation was not affected; in fact, increased consumption spending appears to have created more (part-time) jobs.

It isn't rational to expect significant numbers of people to stop working, since the BIG would replace all wage income only for a very small fraction of workers. The vast majority want more than that and would still have plenty of opportunity and incentive to keep working. And a UBI would actually increase work incentives because, unlike unemployment benefits that they would likely replace, they do not disappear upon return to work. In addition, the free choice element of UBI improves workers' emotional and physical well-being, which are significant factors in productivity. Removing the stigma of "unemployed" that comes with benefits under the current system helps create a society of perceived equals, which in turn improves trust and motivation (Hammond 2017, Hugill and Franklin 2017).

What people do with their benefit is none of our business; that's what "unconditional" means. Some will undoubtedly make poor choices. But that does not justify withholding choice or making choices for those in need – a policy that doesn't protect anyone and yet harms everyone seeking assistance. We can hope it not only helps those with little or no other resources acquire adequate shelter, food, and health care, but that it ultimately helps them obtain employment, because that's the key to living above a subsistence level. It should provide many more choices by removing some of the pressure to accept a bad job and by supplementing whatever wages and benefits are realized.

---

[19] In addition to concern about dependency on handouts, conservatives object to basic income schemes out of concern the money will be misused, for example to fund drug habits. Evans and Popova (2014) reviewed 30 studies on the subject and found no evidence that unconditional transfers increased alcohol and tobacco use.

Some employers will be tempted to capture the income guarantee for themselves by reducing compensation. This may help keep some self-employed individuals in business. Others may have to offer higher wages than before to people who no longer have to accept less to meet basic needs and/or satisfy public assistance work requirements. We don't know how it will play out, and the only thing we can be sure of is that millions of labor relationships will be affected. Not everyone (and maybe no one) will be satisfied. However, they will find it difficult to support a claim that a generous infusion of unconditional income has made low wage workers or their employers worse off.

Atonement and No Adult Left Behind

A robust safety net like SSBI will accomplish two very important social goals: It will help those who have been harmed or disadvantaged by past policies, and it will offer some protection to those who experience misfortune or find themselves disadvantaged by future policy choices. Because SSBI is just one of many variants of BIG, it will be better understood if the concept is clear; this section will provide an overview.

Public policy is messy business. It's impossible to satisfy everyone and a defining feature of good compromise is that no one is entirely pleased. The US political system is designed for inefficient but inclusive decision-making that yields highly imperfect laws and regulations. They tend to provide something for all major stakeholders but may be as inefficient to implement and administer as they were to enact. From introduction of a bill to annual budgets and reporting, it all looks a lot more like sausage-making than choreographed ballet, so it should come as no surprise that even those who were supposed to benefit find themselves worse off or just left behind. Congress uses its scarce oversight opportunities to engage in partisan theatrics that either 1) berate someone for not doing what the current majority party expected of them, or 2) build a case for bills they intend to introduce soon. Its main objective is a show of power, not analysis of what has worked, what has not worked, and why. Congress has demonstrated virtually no willingness or capability to admit that policy is merely theory; that we need evidence to determine whether or not it achieved stated objectives, and that the policy should be reversed or amended if it proves ineffective. We lurch from one bill to another in a partisan game of whack-a-mole that leaves bureaucrats and citizens to live with the unintended consequences (Richardson 2011: 1-5, 21-2).

Ideally, we'd elect representatives with extraordinary understanding of our complex system of government and an equally extraordinary commitment to learning from policy mistakes. That will not happen in my lifetime, so while we work on that, wouldn't it make sense to enact an insurance policy – a failsafe to protect the millions of innocent victims? Let the Wall Street and Washington suits bludgeon one another over monetary and fiscal policy. I would prefer they do battle in a truly free market, but we are as far from that as we are from the electoral ideal. It doesn't matter which industry or firm wins or loses protection; until we are able to remove the cash and prizes altogether, at the very least we should see that those least able to weather the storms are held harmless by a BIG.

Other challenges loom, such as technological change. Experience so far in this century is that the pace is accelerating, and the data presented in Chapter 2 suggest that its effects are felt keenly by those at the bottom of the income distribution – people who have already endured decades of neglect at best and exploitation at worst. We can see more waves coming, so the question is whether we wait for the tsunami of unemployment to hit or prepare for it. Waiting would be tragic because it could lead to strong political resistance to job losses that stops progress in its tracks and denies tremendous opportunities (Frey 2019: 331). Since we will not have time to accurately predict impacts and develop effective policy responses, we must design a broad-based policy that is flexible enough to protect anyone who might lose out, thereby paving the way for businesses to experiment with labor saving technologies. The gains must exceed the losses *to society* because the public safety net will have to be funded by tax increases.

Such foresight would be a game-changer for our country. For far too long, capitalists have managed to pocket huge profits while dispersing their costs and losses among the many US working stiffs. They will claim that a BIG creates a leisure class that will live at the expense of hard-working entrepreneurs. What it actually does is compensate people who were and are left behind in part by choices others have made. They will have the choice of what to do with what little is provided at public expense – payments that may not even come close to restitution for past damages. It's literally the least we can do, because morality and politics lead to the same conclusion: We cannot allow development of technologies that eliminate the livelihood of millions of Americans. As Yuval Noah Harari (2018: 35-7) notes, we need to "honestly acknowledge that the social, economic, and political models we have inherited from the past are inadequate for dealing with such a challenge." New models "should be guided by the principle of protecting humans rather than jobs. Many jobs are uninspiring drudgery and not worth saving. Nobody's dream is to be a cashier. We should focus instead on providing for people's basic needs and protecting their social status and self-worth."

BIG is not new; it has been debated – even in Congress – for at least 50 years. Yet the idea has survived and even grown in popularity as other solutions to poverty continue to fail. Those unfamiliar with BIG raise the same questions asked in the 1970's, such as "Why would people work if their incomes were guaranteed? How can the United States afford it? Why should you and I work to support welfare chiselers? Why can't everyone get a job?" (Sheahen 2012: 1-2). These and other questions are answered in a primer on BIG that includes the following points:[20]

- "When we say we need more jobs, what we really mean is we need more money to live on." (26)

- "The same people who want to cut welfare spending are often the ones who enjoy another type of welfare. Some of them call it defense contracts. If they're in universities, they call it research grants. If they're farmers, they call it farm subsidies. If they're corporations, they call it loan guarantees." (28)

- BIG boosts consumption of goods and services, which stimulates the economy. It will help eliminate the division of our society into those who pay and those who receive public funds. Husbands won't have to leave home so their families qualify for welfare. People could afford to move to where the jobs are or stay in a small town where they can afford to live. It would cut crime. (57-8)

- Not everyone will use the helping hand of BIG to engage in productive activity. So what? We have freeloaders under our current system but do not punish the vast majority who need help to deny the few who take advantage. And we should be very careful about playing God by judging who "deserves" assistance. (62-5)

- There are many ways to pay for the BIG (e.g., by replacing the "hodgepodge of paternalistic and inadequate welfare programs" and cutting tax expenditures). But it could also help us avoid enormous expenses caring for or imprisoning people who were victimized by poverty as children. (94-5)

- Most people will seek work to supplement the BIG because it will not support more than a bare subsistence. Moreover, evidence indicates most of us need work to feel useful and to live meaningful lives. (98-9)

---

[20] Page numbers in Sheahen (2012) are in parentheses at the end of each bullet.

Chapter 4. Moral Inventory

[B]ecause all citizens – not only the poor – become recipients of benefits, people in the middle class come to approach their government as claimants, not as self-governing citizens, and to approach the social safety net not as a great majority of givers eager to make sure that a small minority of recipients are spared from devastating poverty but as a mass of dependents demanding what they are owed. It is hard to imagine an ethic better suited to undermining the moral basis of a free society.

– Yuval Levin (2011)

This very pointed statement about the moral and fiscal bankruptcy of Social Security and Medicare appears in an essay challenging conservatives to develop a vision for making America's "wealth and promise accessible to all." Levin calls for reforms that eliminate most tax deductions and exclusions (especially employer-based health insurance), transition to means-testing of federal retirement benefits, and limiting federal social welfare programs to block grants for states – all designed to help those who need it while restoring independence to those who do not. My SSBI proposal, while not exactly what he has in mind, also simplifies taxes and administration while focusing assistance.

We cannot even consider BIG without addressing the issue of work. It's worth noting that before we even had a welfare state in the US, Bertrand Russell (1932) challenged the cultural assumption that we need to justify our existence through labor:

From the beginning of civilization until the Industrial Revolution, a man could, as a rule, produce by hard work little more than was required for the subsistence of himself and his family…. The small surplus above bare necessaries was not left to those who produced it, but was appropriated by warriors and priests…. At first, sheer force compelled them to produce and part with the surplus. Gradually, however, it was found possible to induce many of them to accept an ethic according to which it was their duty to work hard, although part of their work went to support others in idleness…. The conception of duty, speaking historically, has been a means used by the holders of power to induce others to live for the interests of their masters rather than for their own.

Modern methods of production make it possible to keep most people in relative comfort with less work, but instead of reducing labor, the "Slave State" takes advantage of workers by changing the basis of wages from production to hours of "virtuous" labor. The rich "preach the dignity of labor, while taking care themselves to remain undignified in this respect." We could enjoy ease and security for all, he says, but have chosen instead to overwork some people and starve others.

No one has a right to another's labor. We abolished slavery, yet we seem OK with taking advantage of those who lack better options than to work for us and withholding taxes from paychecks to pay for our one-size-fits-all retirement plan. It's none of our business, as a matter of public policy, whether an individual works, or not. No one owes anyone else a job, either, but if we continue to insist on jobs as the only means to food and shelter, we should expect the poor to clamor for jobs, hours, and minimum wages.

Those who find joblessness morally repugnant or welfare burdensome may reply that taxing income to pay for a BIG is the same thing in reverse – giving those not working (or not earning enough) a claim on the labor of those who are more productive. But it's not the same, at all. First of all, especially with a BIG in place, those who work choose to do so, in full knowledge that their earnings will be taxed to pay for many things they do not personally approve of. Second and more importantly, the BIG is social insurance – meaning those who are paying now could just as easily have received benefits last year or need them next year. All of us who pay insurance premiums hope we never file a claim. Likewise, we should gladly pay a small surtax to support a program we never intend to rely upon. We should be able to agree in principle that we want to live in a society with a safety net – a policy or set of measures that protects all members from misfortune.[21] SSBI is a vehicle for implementing such a policy, and it is too "big" of a change to rush or attempt passage by stealth. Its design is flexible enough to allow for passage by consensus, with an understanding that Congress can amend the details (generosity of payments and tax profile for funding) as needed.

It's all welfare. Every bit of it. Whether it's appropriated or classified as a tax expenditure, any commitment of federal funds redistributes wealth and some of us

---

[21] This is Rawls' (1971) theory that political institutions should be designed behind a "veil of ignorance" as to whether we are or will become privileged or disadvantaged.

win or lose more than others. Some claim, self-righteously, that doing more for the poor will take us down the slippery slope of a welfare state. We took that step a long time ago, and because – as I have shown – federal transfers have favored the rich, we should not be surprised that income inequality is growing. The folly, not to mention the unfairness, of continuing such policies is obvious. Reversing the flow is not introducing a new function of government; it's a course correction.

We're tearing our country apart with mean, pointless arguments about who deserves what from whom. Just the fact that we're debating these issues belies the myth that our economic system is fundamentally different from those in Europe, Asia, or elsewhere. Our Constitution is unique but most original provisions have been ignored or rationalized out of any meaningful effect. The political party that claims belief in limited government has abandoned any credible attempts to limit spending and other measures of federal power and influence. We've been redistributing wealth on a massive scale for a century while maintaining a narrative that our system is better than those of countries with Socialist parties because we don't have one. Now that a few politicians have dared to admit they are Socialist, conservatives are actually thrilled to have a foil for their own extremism.

If we don't chill out and grow up, i.e., stop treating socialism like the bogeyman, every election will be a choice between demagogues. We are capable of governing ourselves; acting like it means having serious, nuanced conversations about what we want for our society. "Socialist" has been used as a malicious label for people associated with vaguely defined notions of "far left" or "very liberal." The sad thing is that – as is common with labels – most people using the term don't really know what it means, and the people they think are socialists may not know or care. In most cases, the only purpose served is alienation.

As an economic term, socialism means government ownership of the means of production – capital and labor. Communist China and Soviet Russia are the most prominent examples. Both abandoned the purely socialist features of their systems after massive failures in the 20th century. Advanced democratic countries, mostly in Europe, were never socialist in the strict sense of the term; they just have more services provided by the state than we do here in the US. Many of these policies reflect preferences of political parties that call themselves social democrats or democratic socialists to indicate they are, as we would say, "liberal" or "progressive" because they strongly support government provision for basic needs such as food, housing, health care, and education. We have very large federal programs for all of these things, so differences are more in method than ideology.

Unfortunately, the mere suggestion that we would have single payer health care or any other "socialist" safety net – and its attendant taxation – gets the tea party crowd's blood boiling. Hysteria serves demagogues but not our democracy. We should not fear any serious proposals presented in good faith. Instead, we should be more trusting of one another and highly skeptical of any pundit or politician who accuses the opposition of threatening destruction.

For perspective on this topic, consider the worst examples of what socialist leaders wrought, such as Stalinist Russia and Fascist Germany. In 1917, Bolshevik communists overthrew the monarchy in Russia with support of peasants who had suffered for centuries to feed their families while Czarist rulers used the fruits of their labor to build luxurious palaces. Of course, the promised equality did not materialize. Communist Party members enjoyed privileges while, under Josef Stalin's reign of terror, they imprisoned and killed millions of their countrymen on the pretense that they were threats to the regime. In 1929, Adolf Hitler's National Socialists (Nazis) seized power in Germany with enthusiastic support of proud people whose defeat in World War I was followed by humiliation and suffering due to sanctions imposed by the Allied victors. His egomaniacal ambitions were fueled by genocide; the Nazis' Holocaust murdered millions of Jews.

These awful historical experiences illustrate the irony in claims that "socialist" welfare policies will destroy work, because in both cases, workers were the heart and soul of Socialist party doctrine and propaganda. Stalin built a vast network of labor camps that were supposed to reform criminals and political prisoners by teaching them the value of work (Solzhenitsyn 1974).[22] Hitler's most famous concentration camp, Auschwitz, featured a welcome arch with the words "Arbeit Macht Frei," which means "work sets you free." I'm not suggesting there is any similarity whatsoever between the American work ethic and Soviet or Nazi prisons; I am saying we should learn a few simple lessons that millions of people paid for with their lives:

1. Avoid labeling or judging anyone as socialist or fascist, because that just divides us and presents an opportunity for very dangerous "leaders."

2. Be extremely careful about the use of force, especially when it comes to labor. Slavery comes to mind.

3. Listen very carefully to what people are saying about inequality, because when push comes to shove, we risk a bloody revolution that nobody actually wins.

---

[22] This is just an extreme case of what Guy Standing (2016: 8) calls "labourism," a merit system in which those who perform certain types of work enjoy privileges or avoid punishment as compared to those who do not.

It's about time we stopped trying so hard to claim the moral high ground to justify our own tax breaks, treat others as if they are coasting on our dime, and even pretend we are doing them a favor by forcing them to work. Our worship of work has been used to rationalize extreme income inequality as the result of a merit system; this is blaming the victims of a relentless pursuit of public policies that confer advantages to those with the means to purchase elections.

Employment status is fair game for creditors, and an individual's work experience, capability, and production history are definitely the business of an employer. But it has taken on far more importance in our judgmental, competitive, class-conscious culture. "What do you do?" means whom do you work for. Since many of us spend most of our waking hours working or commuting and may actually have interesting jobs or careers, that can be an innocent icebreaker. But it is also the primary data point for determining social status. For that reason, we can be tempted to pretend we are more happy or successful than we really are. And if we happen to be "between jobs," some of us hide it behind a claim that we are "consulting."

Derek Thompson (2019) calls this "workism" and its adherents *Homo Industrious*. Rich American men, mostly, have come to believe that "work is not only necessary to economic production, but also the centerpiece of one's identity and life's purpose… and any policy to promote human welfare must *always* encourage more work." His concern is that this "pathological" obsession is setting up Millennials for disappointment, and he endorses solutions like the BIG that would make it easier to resist the pressure to work long hours.

I'm more concerned about the effect of workism on public policy; workaholics are free to indulge but their habits are not good for society as a whole. Work can be a source of pride, but only for the worker. Those who employ labor may lay claim to the tangible results, but the sense of accomplishment, of having done a good job, of making a contribution, of demonstrating skill, overcoming obstacles, creating or learning something new – all of that belongs to the person who actually did the work. Few real achievements are solitary; those feelings are often shared among colleagues or partners. Just as real are the equally deserved feelings associated with not having done a job one promised to do, of carelessness or negligence, not pulling one's weight, etc. Merit is real and valid as a basis for reward or punishment by those with skin in the game. We're all entitled to our opinions about others' choices of whether to work, how much, at which occupation, under what conditions, with and for whom. However, it is not our business simply because we pay or have paid taxes.

We should be very concerned about the ethics that guide public policies. Instead of trying to squeeze as much labor as possible out of people who are at the mercy of the state, we should be protecting their freedom and dignity. Let's do what we can to provide everyone ample opportunity to earn a good wage or run their own business while respecting their right to make other choices – just as we respect their right to marry, raise children, worship, seek higher education, and live where and with anyone they please. Let's not pretend those of us with means enjoy moral superiority that confers the right to condemn those without means to work for us – or for others like us – as if to pay a penalty for their past mistakes or misfortune.

What we really need is humility. Americans are far too proud of how hard we work and far too quick to claim that we earned all the wealth, health, and other privileges we enjoy. There is some truth to that story; even if the game is rigged for or against certain classes of people, some fare better or worse than others in similar circumstances precisely because they did or did not invest their own blood, sweat, and tears. But winners don't need recognition or additional rewards. They need what we all need, which is elevation of the spirit. That happens by demonstrating what we knew all along or learned on our journey to success about being better human beings. A helping hand is not extended reluctantly, as we seem to regard welfare in this country. It's giving back and paying forward – terms commonly used to describe philanthropy but almost never in reference to public programs. There are many problems with our social services, but none of them will be solved by blaming the people who rely on them. Instead of asking whether they deserve help, we should act like we deserve what we have. A generous social safety net demonstrates that we appreciate our gifts enough to share them with others.

Our Ill-conceived Workfare Maze

In today's economy, the assumption that anyone and everyone can obtain a decent job is cruel. Yet it shapes eligibility criteria for all major federal assistance programs. We have a rather strong preference for attaching conditions to limit cost and to encourage independence. We have succeeded in controlling the cost of benefit programs but that does not mean participants' needs were met or that social costs were avoided. In fact, stingy poverty relief program designs meant to limit eligibility for income support can harm intended beneficiaries.

Earnings limits, for example, raise the marginal cost of work and lead to dependency. It is not hard to see why such strategies fail. Eligible individuals rationally avoid work or sever ties to family members who do. When such rules prompt a father to leave his children with their mother, there are at least two bad economic consequences: the living arrangement is inefficient and the broken household makes it more likely the younger generation will remain poor. And those forced into labor have not necessarily achieved financial independence. Policies that make law-abiding citizens work for a "job creator" to earn benefits might be considered a form of human trafficking. It is worse for those who break the law; we commonly make prisoners work to offset the cost of their incarceration. Another curious policy is jailing people who cannot pay fines. What purpose does that serve? For small debts, incarceration amounts to selectively harsh punishment for those who are unemployed. Keeping them locked up doesn't help them pay the debt or find a job upon release, and the expense punishes taxpayers, as well.

Poverty in America is hardly acknowledged, let alone taken seriously. This is supposedly the land of opportunity, so if anyone is suffering, it must be their own fault. Food stamps are still a mark of shame, and anecdotes of people on public assistance living well evoke outrage. To those of us who don't qualify, public benefits appear generous because we see the similarities (what they buy at the grocery store) but not differences (where they live). We also tend to attribute our own tax payments to these individuals. This is all emotion, not reason, and it can all be traced to the mythical work ethic. Wage work is a pillar of a civic religion with roots in the ancient tale of Adam and Eve's punishment and redemption (Block and Piven 2016). Since the Middle Ages, poor relief has been as much about degradation as assistance. Andy Beckett (2018) adds, "Work is the master of the modern world. For most people, it is impossible to imagine society without it. It dominates and pervades everyday life – especially in Britain and the US – more completely than at any time in recent history…. And yet work is not working, for ever more people, in ever more ways. We resist acknowledging these as more than isolated problems – such is work's centrality to our belief systems – but the evidence of its failures is all around us."

Tying assistance to past or future work is not ethical policy. It is judgmental. The American people have not become lazy. They are playing a game of musical chairs for good jobs designed by the one percenters, who have found a way to get rich without employing much labor. It's evil to pretend we are helping someone by giving them a job when that is the only way they can survive. Proposals to guarantee jobs are wasteful and do nothing to address the injustice of such an attitude. And shaming people into work is not working. An enlightened public policy would replace the class-based, sanctimonious notion that work is noble with an honest recognition that work is primarily a means to consumption. Instead of shaming people who don't work, we should help those who do, and focus on alleviating poverty.

Welfare-to-work policies have not reduced poverty (Weissman 2016), but politicians continue to push them because they believe work is a duty for citizens and a resource we have elected them to manage (Dewey and Jan 2017, Badger 2017). They suggest that those who are not working are lazy, that if employers cannot fill positions, it is because no one is qualified, and that workers' lack of qualifications is a problem public institutions should solve. No wonder we have a system that is carefully designed to make all able-bodied persons "earn" their keep and hypocritically avoids subjecting those with means (plenty of *unearned* income) to the same indignities (Bach 2017, Alston 2018: 6, 10).

TANF was designed to reduce poverty by encouraging work, but any effects it may have had on employment appear to be more a consequence of limiting aid; benefits are revoked after 2 years from those deemed able to work. Its most significant result was shifting child support costs from governments to non-custodial parents. Block and Piven (2016) fault TANF for its "arduous and insulting" conditions that require people to "submit to innumerable bureaucratic routines that teach the lesson that wage work, any wage work, is preferable to the dole."

SNAP, more commonly known as the food stamp program, has been targeted for work requirements that are unlikely to be effective at anything other than adding billions of dollars in training expenses and an enormous administrative burden to states (Wolkomir and Dean 2018). Research indicates that work requirements have not lifted aid recipients out of poverty, even if they found jobs. And most able-bodied, working age Medicaid and SNAP recipients are already working. People who are eligible for these benefits already lose access for administrative reasons such as lost notices and administrative errors; adding work requirements will likely increase those risks (Hahn 2018). Butcher and Schanzenbach (2018) analyzed labor market data for SNAP and Medicaid beneficiaries and found that most of them were working substantial hours at low wages that did not grow for fifteen years. Especially since their work is volatile (by nature of occupations), they may find it difficult to meet work requirements to continue receiving benefits they have used to make ends meet.

Behavioral scientists at Ideas42 faulted the Trump Administration's efforts to expand work requirements for food and housing assistance and medical coverage for violating poverty reduction core principles. Living in poverty means dealing with chronic scarcity, a condition in which challenges pile up and force decisions based on immediate needs. Poor people need simplification, "slack," and empowerment; work requirements add hassles, impose rigid schedules, and reinforce stigmas. In June 2018, Arkansas became the first state to implement the Administration's waiver program by imposing work requirements on Medicaid recipients. In a matter of months, the requirement of 80 hours per month in job-related activity (including school, volunteering, and job search) caused 18,000 people (of about 20,000 to whom the new requirement applied) to lose coverage. Mission accomplished?

The notion of earning benefits has influenced programs of all kinds at all levels of government. For example, the Worcester (Massachusetts) Housing Authority requires residents who are not over 55 or disabled go to work or school to avoid eviction (Semuels 2015). The policy, which was intended to reduce dependence and encourage self-sufficiency, began with case management assistance. But that did not work, even after it was expanded to include new applicants (not just residents). Some participants appreciate the help, but others object to intrusive practices such as comments on relationships. And the requirement stands even if residents are current on rent payments. Officials are convinced that the program is working. As long as there are enough applicants willing to participate, that will be true by definition – just like the welfare reforms of the 1990s successfully reduced dependence by removing those who were unable or unwilling to comply with work requirements.

Oren Cass (2013) argued that an effective safety net can encourage work if marginal tax rates are low, i.e., if beneficiaries retain most of what they earn as they enter the workforce. The tangled web of state and federal programs is poorly integrated, and conflicts can lead to disqualification with small increases in income.[23] Cass advocates distinguishing income support from workforce development programs to increase the income gap – the incentive to work provided by significantly higher take-home pay vs. welfare benefits. He further recommends limiting the federal role to providing block grants that allow states to allocate funds between the two types of programs based on local needs. Finally, Cass cites the absurdity of imposing work requirements for food stamp recipients; not only does this mean we would literally deny people access to food, but it accepts as normal a situation where people with jobs still need food stamps!

Ed Dolan's (2018) research indicates work requirements are ineffective: "[T]o the extent work requirements have any statistically significant effects, they both increase time worked and decrease public benefits received. As a result, they have an ambiguous effect on total household income, since additional income earned may not offset the loss of public benefits. This may count as a policy success if the goal is reducing public outlays. But it makes work requirements a problematic tool for

---

[23] More recently, a study of decisions to enter the labor force that featured focus groups in Virginia, Ohio, and California found that participants in TANF, SNAP, and child care and rental assistance programs consider increasing their earnings a risk due to instability of income and uncertainty of getting benefits restored if they lose their job or otherwise experience a reduction in earnings (Chien et al. 2021).

combating poverty among households with able-bodied but low-skill workers." There are several reasons for the failure. Sharp reduction of benefits with increasing income (to save money and target the poor) reduces the incentive to work.[24] Also, jobs cannot be accessed on demand; many of those willing to work face barriers such as child care or transportation needs, disabilities, criminal records, addiction, and low skills. Moreover, the complex and changing nature of work for this population make eligibility determination, proper counseling and coordination with service providers, and tracking difficult for administrators who are chronically underfunded.

As the film *I, Daniel Blake* so effectively illustrated, navigating the workfare bureaucracy can be demeaning, infuriating, and ultimately tragic. While the setting for this story is England, the system and characters could easily be American. The story revolves around Daniel, 59 years old and disabled, trying to satisfy onerous work search requirements. As one reviewer described it, the movie shows how the process dehumanizes service providers as well as applicants, and how "[welfare] funds are dispersed and utilized… in a horrifically inefficient, bureaucratic, lunatic, dehumanising, hopeless, helpless fashion" (Roberts et al. 2016).

Elizabeth Breunig (2018) points to the hypocrisy of those who continue to support work requirements for public assistance. While a mere two percent of America's poor are able-bodied adults who choose not to work, those with incomes over $10 million received just 15 percent of it from salaries; the rest is interest, dividends, capital gains, etc. And while entitlements such as Social Security and Medicare are frequently cited as causing runaway federal spending, tax expenditures for the same purposes that benefit the wealthy (pension and health insurance benefits) to the tune of several hundred billion dollars each year do not seem to be cause for concern. Special tax treatment of capital gains adds insult to injury by favoring people who have money to invest over those struggling to make ends meet.[25] As Piketty (2017: 423) notes, tax reductions for the rich act as an "amplifying mechanism," whereby the proceeds of their conquests are invested in further political influence. At the very least, we can remove preferential tax treatment of unearned income.

Look more closely at our apparent obsession with work, and we find it isn't really about work per se; it's about earnings. We expect people to pay their own way, and

---

[24] See Figure 3.2. Welfare benefits are just one of many factors, but clearly work requirements exacerbate the problem of high marginal tax rates faced by low-income households.

[25] Correcting imbalances in tax treatment of wages vs. unearned income is a prominent feature of my proposed reforms. Guy Standing (2016: xii) refers to people who derive most of their income from property and other assets as "rentiers." He claims they have corrupted not just capitalism, but democracy, as well.

it so happens that for most of us, the only way that is possible is via paid employment. This is why it's OK if wealthy people and retirees don't work, but we frown upon the unemployed. We accept ability to pay as evidence of earnings, hence merit. All of this means the real obstacle to radical reforms like UBI is cultural, not economic, and that hurdle can be overcome if we let go of the idea that security and social status must be earned through employment (Klein 2016). We're more likely to consider and adopt humane policies if we remember that we're dealing with complex human beings. Each has more to offer than wage labor and we should not judge them by their employment status. UBI can supplement or substitute wage income, but it can also serve as a vehicle for self-determination and human development. A basic income rewards contributions to society that go beyond narrow cash terms, such as reciprocity, community service, and family support (Painter and Thuong 2016).

While conservatives tend to view social insurance as a threat, it was recognized long ago as a proactive defense of private property (Anderson 2016). Thomas Paine proposed such programs as a more humane solution to poverty than the English Poor Laws that subjected the poor to degrading inquiries, work requirements, and social stigma. The basis of his scheme was a belief that Earth is common property; his proposal was to impose a 10 percent inheritance tax on landowners to fund universal old-age pensions, disability insurance, and stakeholder grants for young adults. Since everyone could claim the benefit, no one would be "forced to forgo their liberty as a condition of subsistence." The alternative, he warned, might be a communist revolution, which at that time was a serious threat in France.

Ironically, conservative icon Friedrich Hayek argued that the state should guarantee everyone a basic level of income security funded by general revenues (as opposed to the Bismarck-style programs funded by payroll taxes and favored by the middle class). He leveled several criticisms of US entitlements: 1) Younger generations will not support generous payments to the elderly indefinitely, 2) Tying benefits to payroll taxes denies people choices in current vs. future consumption they should make for themselves, 3) The state should not grade benefits (another link to taxes paid) based on who "deserves" them, 4) The insured event is falling into poverty, so benefits should be means-tested, and 5) Reference to "earned" benefits is fraudulent because the system actually redistributes income "from the young and lucky to the old and unlucky."

Many in what we call the "working class" are too proud to accept handouts. They may be dissatisfied with their situation but feel superior to those unable or unwilling to work. It's hard to think of an issue that draws more righteous indignation than working for a living while others are idle and get paid, anyway. And this is why they often side with the one percent to oppose "unearned" benefits. There are a host of other reasons Americans may find it difficult to accept a BIG solution. Ideologically, libertarians believe taxation for purposes such as redistribution is theft and conservatives believe welfare programs destroy character by rewarding sloth. Those who do not feel obligated to aid the poor may think it's more properly done by voluntary institutions, and those who believe income support harms beneficiaries may be more interested in dismantling existing welfare programs than improving them. In other words, not everyone is on board with the role of government in social welfare. This actually strengthens the argument for close scrutiny of what we're doing, why we're doing it, and whether it is working.

We need to look in the mirror when speaking of handouts. Fortunately, most of us have not had to apply for food stamps, subsidized housing, or TANF benefits. But that doesn't mean we are financially independent. Income tax exemptions for children and deductions for mortgage interest are just two of the most common benefits that together exceed, per household, so-called welfare payments. Many of us feel entitled to these tax breaks because we earned the money; never mind that taxes are higher for others earning the same incomes. And don't we reelect representatives who steer federal money to our communities? We should not look down on the poor for relying on public assistance when we all do it to some degree.

Fair Wages

Any labor exchange presents an array of relative values and ethics. Who gets to determine what is and isn't fair? Value of work is not the business of government. Individuals and employers should be free to choose; public policy should be neutral on whether, how, and how much people work and are paid for it. Yes, this means minimum wage laws are wrong as a matter of principle because they violate the rights of employers and workers to negotiate wages. They're also wrong because they do harm by reducing employment of low-wage workers (US CBO 2019). Society is then burdened with assisting those who were priced out of the market.

Oren Cass (2018) observes that minimum wage laws hide the cost of public policy by imposing those costs on employers and workers. He argues that a better way to help workers with insufficient earnings is to do so directly through a subsidy that would allow employers to hire workers at wages higher than they are willing to pay. He says "lessening the social distinction between idleness and productive activities is not an enhancement of freedom but rather a form of deprivation" and "well-meaning effort to elevate the status of people who fail to provide for themselves, or at least insulate them from reproach, has the unavoidable consequence of reducing or erasing any 'respect gap' between idleness and work" (Cass 2018: 158-9, 172-3, 202). I agree with much of what he has to say. However, his wage subsidy is designed to close a perceived production deficit, not to help the poor, and it amounts to a doubling down on policy failures that add insult to injury. Forcing people into jobs so they can earn respect will not set them free. They already deserve respect, which we should demonstrate by offering unconditional assistance that allows them to choose freely whether and how to pursue higher objectives.

Making paid work the only practical means of obtaining food and shelter while making credit free to those with assets has created an economy that favors "job creators" (i.e., saviors) who should not be subjected to annoying regulation, taxes, or competition, lest they cut off sustenance to prospective workers. People facing eviction or hunger can hardly be considered free agents. An effective safety net would help offset employers' advantageous bargaining power by placing a floor on wages, one worker at a time. If basic needs are not at stake, people would not have to accept jobs they don't want and they would have leverage to negotiate terms of employment (hours, wages, benefits, and other conditions). The basic income "would act as a kind of twenty-first century union." Many low-income workers already rely on public assistance programs such as Medicaid, children's health insurance, food stamps, and the Earned Income Tax Credit (Lowrey 2018a: 52-3). Especially when eligibility for public benefits requires work, employers do not have to offer higher wages to attract or keep their employees. Imagine how that dynamic would change if income support was unconditional. All workers would have their basic needs covered, so an employer could not count on a line of desperate job applicants for part-time, minimum wage jobs. "Job creators" might actually have to offer good jobs.[26]

Today's employers complain about not having enough workers with the right skills. To the extent jobs do require specific skills, employers have not shown much interest in paying for them (Sawhill 2018). Roosevelt Institute scholars find little evidence of a skills gap. They find it more likely "pervasive and inherent" monopsony (buying power) in the labor market allows employers to "look for more and better workers while paying low wages and refusing to raise them." In any event, government funded education and training programs abound. Unfortunately, returns on such investments are inconsistent and do not always benefit workers because

---

[26] Tax credits actually hold down wages and weaken workers' bargaining power. They subsidize employers and reduce productivity and competitiveness by encouraging use of lower value work (Standing 2016: 109-12).

increased productivity tends to be captured by employers. Workers need more than skills in this market; they need bargaining power. For this reason, the authors recommend delivery of training in partnership with labor unions and nonprofit organizations that can assist workers in obtaining better outcomes (Naidu and Sojourner 2020: 4-5).

Another study published by the Department of the Treasury (2022a: i-ii) finds evidence of monopsony power that limits competition for labor to such an extent that wages are about 20 percent lower than the level that would exist in a fully competitive market. Some advantages are inherent in the employment relationship (e.g., comparable wages, hidden discrimination or unsafe working conditions, coupled with limited ability to find better jobs and even relocate). Other advantages result from deliberate practices such as conspiring to fix wages; no-poach agreements with competing firms; forcing workers to sign non-disclosure, non-compete, and mandatory arbitration agreements; pay secrecy; excessive occupational licensing requirements; and outsourcing/misclassification of contract workers.

Two more examples illustrate what workers face in today's job markets. "In a recent Accenture survey of 1,200 CEOs and other top executives, 74 percent said that they plan to use artificial intelligence to automate tasks in their workplace over the next three years. Yet only three percent reported planning to significantly increase investments in training over the same time period" (McKay, Pollack, and Fitzpayne 2019: 7). Some employers could be hiding sinister motives. The supply of Science, Technology, Engineering, and Math (STEM) graduates is at least twice the demand. Oversupplies of talent increase competition among workers for job openings and reduce demands on employers to entice applicants. On average, 245 candidates apply to each job posted online. The really sad thing is that some of the positions don't even exist (Shell 2018: 168-71).

Why don't employers pay higher wages or fix other impediments to competitiveness? Federal policy is at least partly to blame for making cheap capital available to pursue other options abroad. The Fed's relentless war on interest rates inflated serial bubbles in real estate and financial assets, giving capital an enormous cost advantage over labor and thereby shifting investments away from labor intensive businesses in general and, for manufacturing, toward cheaper foreign sources. In addition, employers are being shortsighted in treating labor as a commodity and seeking to pay as little as possible for performance of mechanical tasks. Prescriptive work rules may effectively control costs and adherence to standards, but they also fail to motivate or reward innovation and loyalty – thereby limiting productivity. Raising wages won't improve poor systems or management practices that negatively impact employee motivation and increase turnover by reducing workers' sense of achievement, pride, and meaning. A more enlightened view of the work environment reveals opportunities to make better use of workers' time and talents (Millerd 2018).

Hourly wage increases don't solve problems of sufficient hours and predictable schedules. That's why millions of Americans have more than one job and may still rely on government assistance. These conditions raise stress levels and adversely affect workers' mental and physical health, which causes performance problems on the job. Workers suffer even lower prospects for better jobs, which in turn leads to high rates of turnover that are very costly to employers. Some employers have found that a "good jobs system" can replace the vicious cycle of low expectations and performance with a virtuous cycle that improves outcomes for customers, employees, and shareholders. Such systems feature five interconnected operational elements: invest in people, focus and simplify, standardize and empower, cross-train, and operate with slack. These companies redesigned frontline jobs to be worth higher pay and developed a system that allowed employees to make them even more valuable to the company. Results include significant improvements in turnover, absenteeism, higher sales, lower costs, and improved productivity (Ton 2023: 11-8, 40-51, 151-2).

Wars and Immigration

As indicated in Chapter 1, I believe the solution to poverty and income inequality in the US lies in understanding the system we've created and taking a deliberate holistic approach instead of continuing the whack-a-mole game of treating symptoms as they arise. In this section, I'll touch on contributions of our national drug policy, military policy, and immigration policy to the problem.

The War on Drugs was supposed to help poor communities by cleaning up the streets. In fact, it has failed miserably because it created a black market that made it easy for criminals to exploit poor young men. Taxes to fight the war soared. Money that could have gone directly to social services went instead to law enforcement and foreign aid. Drug addicts turned to crime to support their habits; the money went to buy luxury goods and weapons sold by the one percent. Whether or not special interests started the war, they are profiting from it and therefore have a strong incentive to keep it going. Data show we're losing, but that doesn't deter those who claim this is a holy war against evil forces.

Alliances between bootleggers and Baptists may have peaked in the Prohibition era, but the sentiment and profitable opportunities persisted.[27] This war has already lasted half a century, despite evidence of systematic failures. "The average inflation-adjusted (and purity-adjusted) prices of heroin, cocaine and cannabis fell by 81%, 80% and 86%, between 1990 and 2007 while average purity increased by 60%, 11% and 161%, respectively" (Chalabi 2016). The implication is clear: Despite massive and increasing efforts to shut down illicit trade in controlled substances, the market is thriving. Meanwhile, monetary and human costs pile on: over $20 billion annually in counter-narcotics expenditures; tens of thousands of Mexicans and Central Americans killed in drug-trafficking; and 350,000 prisoners serving time for drug offenses. In 2010 alone, over 1 million people were arrested for possession, and over half of those arrests were for small amounts of marijuana. Policies oriented toward improving public safety and health would stop the arrest and imprisonment of non-violent users and offer assistance to addicts (Porter 2012).

Some say the war is a tremendous success because its intent was not to eradicate drug abuse but to villainize vulnerable populations, the first being urban blacks and the latest being Hispanic immigrants (Gwynne 2018). Policy responses to the opioid epidemic have typically doubled down on enforcement instead of expanding treatment, despite growing recognition that the "tough on crime" strategy has not worked and that threats from use of drugs like heroin and fentanyl are more about public health than violence. Advocates of new measures targeting dealers equate selling dangerous substances to homicide. They do not understand that many dealers are also addicts who might benefit from treatment and that many of those who overdose got their drugs from a friend or family member. Charging fellow users with murder raises the likelihood of plea deals for harsh prison sentences (Lopez 2017).

Drug abuse is a serious problem that deserves a thoughtful policy response. But until we stop judging victims as irresponsible, undeserving, and even menacing to society, we will fail them and add to the damage their drug use is doing to our society.

Among the reasons for renewed interest in George Orwell's timeless novel *Nineteen Eighty-Four* is appreciation of his insight that perpetual war is an effective means of keeping the lower class ("proles") in line. Machines pose a threat to the hierarchy because they make it possible to eliminate hunger, overwork, illiteracy, and disease. To maintain the balance of power between superstates and more importantly,

---

[27] Bruce Yandle (1983) recognized this model for regulatory entrepreneurs who capture rents by supporting government intervention to address popular concerns. In the titular example, bootleggers helped Baptists close bars and liquor stores on Sunday.

between the ruling class and the working class, wealth must be consumed in production of weapons. "For if leisure and security were enjoyed by all alike, the great mass of human beings who are normally stupefied by poverty would become literate and would learn to think for themselves; and when once they had done this, they would sooner or later realize that the privileged minority had no function, and they would sweep it away…. The very word 'war,' therefore, has become misleading. It would probably be accurate to say that by becoming continuous war has ceased to exist" (Orwell [1949] 1983: 194-204).

When I first heard about the idea of creating the Department of Homeland Security (DHS), I thought it would be redundant to the Department of Defense. In hindsight, I should not have taken either name so literally. Before I was even born (in the 1950s), our leaders had decided the best defense was a potent offense, and that meant maintaining military bases and "Floating Fortresses" (an Orwellian term) all over the globe. It also meant vastly superior nuclear capabilities, an omnipotent intelligence apparatus, a volunteer military force, a constant drumbeat of propaganda, and most importantly, large budget deficits. In hindsight, many Americans question the degree to which we were actually threatened by Communism in general and by the Soviet Union in particular. But in the 1960-90 period, the risk of a nuclear attack – perhaps not on the US mainland but elsewhere, as smaller countries obtained the capability – was plausible. The fall of the Iron Curtain dramatically shifted the balance of power. The arms race was over, but the peace did not last; neither did we see any reduction in "defense" spending.

The rationale for entering Middle East conflicts in the 1980s was protecting oil sources. That is no longer valid, since our supplies today are distributed more broadly. We remain entangled in the region because it benefits the military-industrial complex and the rest of the country is not sufficiently informed or affected to end it. "Reliance on a professional military places the burden of service and sacrifice onto a very small percentage of citizens and lets everyone else off the hook. The resort to deficit spending to underwrite the war's costs sloughs off onto future generations the onus of paying the bills" (Bacevich 2016: 369).

Moreover, our volunteer military force adds to income inequality and other symptoms of institutionalized discrimination by placing the greatest burden of our wars on those with few attractive career alternatives. "Sold by its masterminds as a formula for creating a prosperous and powerful nation in which all citizens might find opportunities to flourish, it has yielded no such thing." The events of 9/11/2001 were calamitous, but they did not constitute or even indicate an existential threat to the United States. They did, however, present an opportunity for Vice President Dick

Cheney, Defense Secretary Donald Rumsfeld, and Deputy Secretary of Defense Paul Wolfowitz to talk President Bush into declaring a War on Terror that – conveniently – provides its own justification and could therefore go on forever. The President described it as a fight for peace and liberty "on every continent" (Bacevich 2020: 108-14, 139-44, 185-6). Orwell's "War is Peace" had come to life.

This sweeping policy has been a boon to those dependent on Defense and DHS spending. But it has taken a toll on others beyond the direct expenditures and even casualties. Many veterans and their families have not fully recovered from physical and mental injuries sustained in the conflicts in the Middle East, and some of them struggle to understand what it was they were fighting for. Most American soldiers come from middle-class families and join military service as an opportunity to (as advertised) be all they can be. But not all make it a career and delivering on the implied promise to help veterans transition to the civilian workforce has been difficult. Defense is a huge program that enriches the one percent at others' expense. Preoccupation with military dominance has caused our leaders to throw caution to the wind with respect to our financial security. Our military policy is morally repugnant and it is a terrific waste of money. I suspect that if forced to choose, most of us would prioritize income security over warmongering.

We all realize and appreciate that the United States of America was built by immigrants, and most of us want to honor and protect that heritage. However, taking that attitude seriously leaves us with a larger problem: Hard-working, law-abiding immigrants take "our" jobs. Protectionism, not security or a more general law enforcement ideal, drives objection to reforms that grant amnesty to illegal immigrants or increase the flow of temporary workers. People who resent free trade or other vehicles of globalization are doubly offended when cheap labor is imported. When that labor enters the market illegally, righteous indignation boils in the emotional cauldron. This attitude runs deep in America, and it is shared by people across the left-right political spectrum.

Redistribution, especially on the scale of a UBI, raises the stakes for a debate on immigration policy that has already proven very difficult. A more generous welfare policy can only attract more immigrants, which makes it even more important to identify citizens and how our rights and benefits differ from those of other residents. Therefore, adoption of UBI in any form is likely to be accompanied by immigration reforms; "voters use immigration policy as an instrument to gain control over redistribution policy" (Ortega 2004).

The widely held opinion that immigrants are a drag on our economy is a myth. The truth is that we are increasingly dependent on them, not only because many of them do work we don't want, but because they are younger, on average. Baby boomer retirements are creating a demographic headwind of increasing dependency on the working age population. The Census Bureau quantifies this as an "old-age dependency ratio" by comparing populations 65 and over with those 18-64 years of age.[28] For the US, this ratio is projected to increase sharply, from 21 (percent) in 2010 to 28 in 2020 and 35 in 2030 before leveling off (Ortman, Velkoff, and Hogan 2014: 9). This means that in just two decades, we will have gone from an economy in which nearly five working age people are available to support each person of retirement age to one in which just three people would bear the same burden. Over roughly the same period, barring dramatic changes in recent trends, it is immigrants who will keep the workforce from shrinking (see Figure 4.1). They will save us from having to bribe our citizens to have more children so we can tax their children later to pay our debts. Even for such selfish reasons, we should welcome immigrants with open arms.

Figure 4.1 Future taxpayers of America

Projected change in the U.S. working-age population, 2015-2035

Ages 25-64, in millions

Group	2015	2035	Change
Immigrants	33.9	38.5	4.6
U.S. born with immigrant parents	11.1	24.6	13.6
U.S. born with U.S.-born parents	128.3	120.1	-8.2
Total	173.2	183.2	10.0

Note: Change calculated before rounding.
Source: Pew Research Center projections.

PEW RESEARCH CENTER

Source: Passel and Cohn 2017

Harry Holzer (2019: 1) adds:

In this context [of rising inequality between skilled and unskilled workers, lower economic growth, and a shrinking workforce], increased immigration can provide many benefits to the U.S. economy. It can benefit consumers by helping reduce the costs and increase the availability of important goods and services, especially

---

[28] They also calculate a youth dependency ratio using the population under 18 in the numerator. It was 38 in 2010 and is projected to remain virtually unchanged through 2050.

those such as health and elder care where demand will rise rapidly as the population ages. Immigration can also contribute some balance to the federal budget as baby boomers retire and pay much lower taxes while drawing heavily on Social Security and Medicare. And finally, it can raise economic growth by replenishing a labor force that would otherwise diminish.

Immigrants are also among the greatest innovators in the U.S. One recent study that compared patents, patent citations, and economic value of patents found that immigrants were responsible for a disproportionate share when compared to native-born inventors. Another study of entrepreneurship found that first-generation immigrants, which make up approximately 14 percent of our population, create 25 percent of all new businesses in the U.S. It's not difficult to understand why; these are people who have endured tremendous risks seeking better opportunities in our country (Tam 2020).

UBI itself is controversial, so we may as well dig deep on what we really want as a society. The social welfare system we have now is clearly communitarian; it prioritizes our right to control membership and take care of our own, meaning the group whose ancestors arrived first. We could replace this seniority system with one that protects those most in need of assistance. While the impact of poor immigrants on the welfare state is not in question, their impact on social welfare is a function of the period chosen for measurement. Immediate redistribution from native workers to employers and immigrants is offset by economic growth that benefits everyone in the long run. Thus, concerns for social welfare do not justify closing our borders (Powell 2006, Jaumotte 2016).

Functional immigration policies would reflect a cosmopolitan, liberal, egalitarian approach in which equal opportunity has precedence over redistribution. A free society would embrace the moral imperative of welcoming hopeful and well-meaning immigrants, commit to their (eventual) full acceptance, and adjust other public policies accordingly. Providing a path to citizenship for illegal immigrants solves a host of problems. It leads to higher wages for them, which reduces their threat to citizens' jobs, increases tax revenue and reduces impact on welfare agencies. There is less need to audit employers for illegal practices connected with undocumented workers. Competition takes place on a level playing field and the transparency of the process allows rapid adjustment to market forces.

Chapter 5. Slaying the Payroll Tax Dragon

America's social welfare policy has become a complex array of taxes and benefits that can be very difficult to analyze. The way forward should be marked by a few guidelines that will help us distinguish good from bad policy options. First, any given provision should lift more people above the poverty line. Second, it should incentivize work. Third, it should reward savings. Finally, and perhaps most importantly, it should treat everyone equally. Listed below are additional, related objectives that guide specific policies described in this chapter:

1. Raise take home pay of poor workers.
2. Relieve the middle class of a tax burden that prohibits real savings they own and control.
3. Let small business owners keep or reinvest earnings.
4. Remove incentives to incur debt.
5. Correct imbalance in treatment of earned vs. unearned income.
6. Cut tax expenditures, which are highly regressive.

Individually and collectively, these are true reforms that will help slow and perhaps reverse the trend of growing income inequality.

Social Security was conceived as a forced savings program designed to help workers invest in their own retirement. But there is no fund and certainly no asset individuals control and pass along to survivors. Workers do not build any wealth and their financial security is entirely under state control. It is actually a redistribution program because workers pay taxes that the government uses to pay obligations to others. Regardless of how we characterize Social Security, it is paternalistic; it deprives workers of the right to act on their own preferences regarding the timing and methods of savings and consumption. The system crushes entrepreneurs; cash flow is dear to any small business, and having to fork over 15 percent of every dollar to the tax man could prevent many of the self-employed from being able to pay bills or make investments needed to survive and grow. For those living on the edge, taxing every dollar they earn makes them more dependent on income support in the future because they find it more difficult to save.

Social Security benefits are determined by contributions, which are tied to earnings. This means those who are least in need of the pension receive the largest benefit payments – a practice that reflects a very strange idea of income security. As the program approaches a full century of operation, benefits as a percentage of contributions are falling, and unless it is radically reformed, we may soon be paying retirees less than they paid into the program. Unless payments are means-tested, we will be punishing those most dependent on the system.

The payroll tax is a suffocating burden on the working poor and small businesses that a real citizens' legislature would recognize as a worthy target for reform. But somehow, Social Security is still considered the third rail of politics long after benefits have been delayed for all, taxed for some, and became widely regarded as a pipe dream for young workers. The regressive nature of the tax is its worst feature, but there are other reasons why we need to fund benefit payments from general revenues, starting now (Capretta 2015, Clancy 2015, and Moon 2023: 304-5). The income tax reform campaign that led to the TCJA targeted marginal tax rates on US corporations. Evidently, in the rush to provide relief to corporations, authors of the legislation did not consider reducing implicit marginal tax rates on the supply of labor – the poverty trap.[29] Thanks to the lockbox myth (treating payroll taxes as savings), analysis of federal taxes on individuals is overwhelmingly focused on the income tax, which is considered fair to low- and middle-income taxpayers because they pay a small percentage of the total (DeSilver 2023). But what really matters is the total tax picture, in which the payroll tax dominates for all lower income workers.[30] That picture is difficult to assemble under the current structure. Our social safety net is in trouble, and we need to have all cards face up on the table if we want to have honest and productive conversations about policy options.

Social Security and Medicare Insolvency

Social Security and Medicare contributions to the federal deficit are projected to grow rapidly over the next 30 years (US CBO 2023b: Table 1-1). "Social Security" refers to the Old-Age, Survivors, and Disability Insurance (OASDI) program established by

---

[29] In addition to the risk of losing benefits that are fragmented and complex, poor people find the payroll tax a barrier to entering the workforce (Dorfman 2015).
[30] In the Tax Policy Center model (2017a), marginal tax rates for the lowest quintile tax units (percent of all filers) are almost entirely due to the payroll tax.

Congress in 1935. Federal payroll taxes of 6.2 percent and 1.45 percent of wages are paid by employers and employees (total 15.3 percent) to fund OASDI and Medicare's Hospital Insurance (HI) program, respectively.

From the mid-1980s until the mid-2000s, OASDI tax revenues exceeded benefits by increasing amounts; since then, costs have risen faster than revenues because retiring baby boomers outnumber younger people entering the workforce. The trust fund balance was still increasing until 2021, when expenditures exceeded revenues by $56 billion (US SSA 2022b: 4.6). Trust fund reserves are projected to reach zero in 2034 for the Old-Age and Survivors Insurance (OASI) and in 2052 for Disability Insurance (DI). Over the 75-year projection period, combined unfunded obligations would grow to *$20.4 trillion* in today's dollars. Eliminating this deficit would require hiking payroll taxes by 3.24 percentage points – from 12.40 percent to 15.64 percent. Alternatively, benefits would have to be reduced by 20.3 percent for all beneficiaries or 24.1 percent for those initially eligible in 2022 or later. Delayed action on these solutions would be even more painful (US SSA 2022a: 3-5).

These are very big numbers that illustrate just how far we have kicked this can down the road. I object to the payroll tax altogether, so obviously I would not recommend raising the rates, and I have a hard time imagining significant support for any increase by those paying the tax, whether or not they believe the program is fundamentally flawed. They do not need to read the Trustees' report. All they need to know is that they're already forking over more for these IOUs than they pay in federal income taxes. Reducing benefits by double digit percentages is completely out of the question. Once upon a time, these programs may have been made whole without drastic changes. At this point, all options entail radical reforms, so it becomes necessary to focus on what is really important and what we are trying to accomplish – which might be considered a silver lining to the cloud.

Several think tanks have tackled the solvency issue. For example, an AEI report on reforming entitlement programs includes a section on Social Security that focuses on providing a safety net for the elderly in the form of a flat benefit at the poverty level. During the very long transition period, no one would lose accrued benefits. Payroll tax funding would continue at a lower rate. The early retirement age would move from 62 to 65, but those still working at 62 would be exempt from the payroll tax (Biggs et al. 2016: 1-4).

A Heritage Foundation report rejects ideas that preserve the current system by raising taxes (Boccia 2017). Payroll tax rates are already high, and they harm those the program is intended to benefit. Raising the cap to which the tax applies (currently $160,200), would drastically increase marginal tax rates and – by extending the short-term surplus generated by OASDI revenues – hide deficit spending in other areas of the budget. Instead, the report suggests, we should address the cash flow problem by revising the cost-of-living adjustment formula, raise the age of eligibility, provide a flat benefit above the poverty line (like the AEI proposal), and phase out payroll taxes. Benefits would be paid from the general fund:

> Since the Trust Fund is merely an accounting mechanism with no real savings to pay Social Security benefits coming due, there would be little harm in eliminating the Trust Fund altogether. US taxpayers are effectively financing Social Security benefits on a pay-as-you-go basis already, as general tax revenues cover the shortfalls between incoming Social Security revenues and outgoing benefits. The absence of this illusory Trust Fund would more likely clear the path for reasonable Social Security reforms. It would enable the nation to recognize the very real and increasing burden on younger generations from unfunded Social Security benefits. It would also reveal the folly of proposals that would create Social Security surpluses in the short run while increasing liabilities over the long run. The Trust Fund creates the on-paper savings while fueling the growth in other areas of government.[31]

Medicare has two trust funds – Hospital Insurance (HI) and Supplementary Medical Insurance (SMI). HI, also known as Medicare Part A, helps pay for hospital, home health services following hospital stays, skilled nursing facility, and hospice care for the aged and disabled. SMI funds voluntary enrollment in Medicare Part B (physician, outpatient hospital, and home health services) and Part D (drug insurance coverage).[32] Depletion of the HI trust fund is projected to occur in 2028. The Board of Trustees' long term (75 year) projection based on current law and intermediate assumptions of workers' earnings is that Medicare expenditures will increase from 3.9 percent of GDP in 2021 ($839.3 billion) to 6.5 percent of GDP in 2096. The report included the following caveat: "Medicare's actual future costs are highly uncertain for reasons apart from the inherent challenges in projecting health care cost growth over time." These reasons stem from provisions of the Affordable Care Act (ACA) and the Medicare Access and CHIP (Children's Health Insurance Program)

---

[31] Historical budget treatment of the trust fund supports Boccia's assessment. It has officially been on- and off-budget for political reasons but almost always included in deficit calculations when its surplus could hide large and/or growing deficits (US SSA 2007). Merging Social Insurance and Retirement accounts into the rest of the federal budget will make our choices more transparent and provide flexibility needed to adjust benefits and taxes.

[32] Medicare Part C is an alternative to coverage under Parts A and B that includes Medicare Advantage and other more comprehensive health insurance plans. Some of its costs are paid for out of the HI and SMI trust funds.

Reauthorization Act (MACRA) that affect payment rates for physicians and other providers. These rates are subject to change and could lead to reduced physician participation (and access to care). Probably due to the complexity of these interrelated, moving parts, the report does not include analysis of funding or program policy alternatives that correspond to the tax or benefit options described above for OASDI (US HHS 2022a: 1-11). However, the Committee for a Responsible Federal Budget (2023) says restoring solvency over the next 75 years would require immediately raising the payroll tax by 21 percent (0.6 percentage points) or reducing spending by 13 percent.

A 2/3 increase in real (percent of GDP) terms over 75 years may not seem to be cause for alarm, except that, as indicated in Figure 5.1 (US HHS 2022a), Medicare expenditures have already doubled in the last 30 years and almost all of the projected growth (50 percent increase) is expected in the next 20 years.

Figure 5.1 Medicare trustees' projection of non-interest income and expenditures as a percentage of the Gross Domestic Product

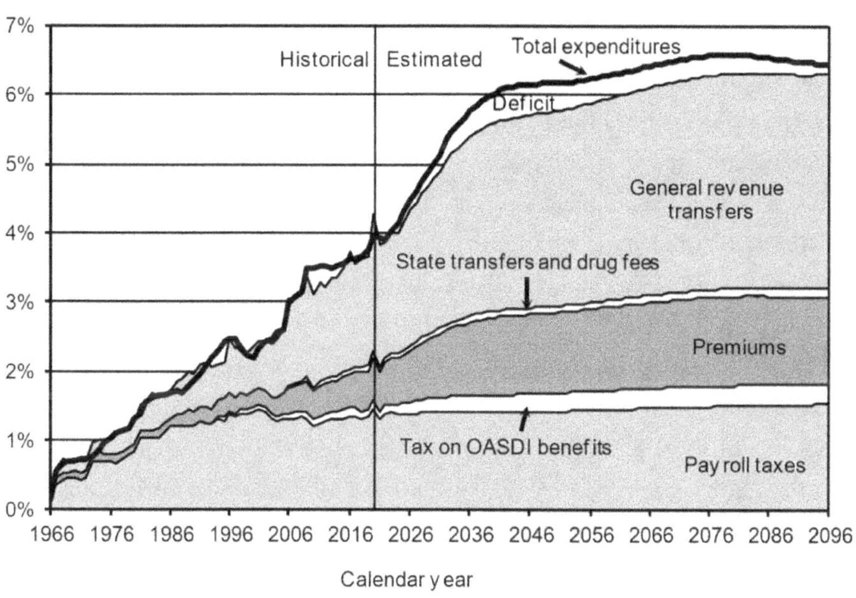

While it is clear that Medicare is in need of attention, thanks to the ACA debates it already has plenty and promises to get even more, with many proposals to expand rather than shrink the program.[33] For the purpose of this book, my only concern with Medicare is the regressive payroll tax. The HI tax collected $303 billion in calendar year (CY) 2021, is a very large amount of money, but far less than OASDI's $984

---

[33] Single payer proposals abound (Neuman, Pollitz, and Tolbert 2018).

billion collected in the same period (US HHS 2022a: 47, US SSA 2022a: 36). If we manage to replace the larger tax, replacing the smaller one becomes much easier. Besides, as Figure 5.1 illustrates, Medicare is already heavily funded by general revenue.

Another reason I'm not targeting Medicare for wholesale reform is that it does not pose nearly the threat to intergenerational inequality. It provides health care services, not cash benefits, that are naturally more in demand by older Americans. They only get what they need. By way of contrast, Social Security payments could help the young as well as the old, and they are not based on need. Medicare, like Social Security, is designed for people over 65, but younger people are not left behind because they have access to Medicaid – a state administered, means-tested health care program jointly funded by state and federal governments.[34, 35]

Eliminating the taxes that are supposed to fund these programs does not eliminate the obligations. It does, however, open up a couple of debates that are long overdue. The first is how the tax code should be amended to replace the revenue stream and the second is how retirement plan benefits will be determined without payroll tax contributions. The revenue question is daunting. Cutting the payroll tax will benefit 179 million American taxpayers and their families who pay it (US SSA 2022a: 2). However, that is very costly and cannot be paid for by taxing others. We have to look at general revenues such as the income tax and how to raise it equitably.

Social Security is a uniquely structured entitlement program. Most programs in the category determine eligibility by applicants' circumstances. With Social Security, benefits are "earned" by payment of taxes and we receive statements each year that quantify what the state owes us. I would call that an obligation. Anyone rejected or cut off from entitlement assistance would be disappointed or upset. But nothing quite compares to the wrath of seniors whose Social Security payments are in jeopardy. Whether or not there is a legal obligation, as a practical matter, there is no question about payment of promised benefits.[36] Shedding existing obligations is off the table for reform, but future obligations are fair game.

---

[34] People who are disabled before reaching retirement age can qualify for Social Security Disability Income (SSDI) and/or Medicare. In CY 2021, SSDI payments were made to 9.2 million workers and their auxiliary beneficiaries (spouses and children) totaling $140 billion (US SSA 2022a: 143, 164). In CY 2021, Medicare served 8.3 million people with disabilities (US HHS 2022a: 8).

[35] The federal commitment is substantial. OMB (2023) estimated FY 2018 Medicaid outlays at $521 billion.

[36] There are no individual rights to benefits, according to the Supreme Court (Boccia 2017).

A campaign to repeal and replace this symbolic institution will make the Affordable Care Act debates look like child's play. At a time when voters and politicians have never been more polarized, proposals from either side of the political spectrum to do much of anything with Social Security will be met with ridicule, vitriol, and more. I'm coming from neither side and therefore, expect to be hit hard by both. That's just the way they roll; the only thing more bipartisan than agreement on more spending may be hatred of independent challengers, whom they refer to as "spoilers." If SSBI or variants receive any attention at all from Congress, it will be a contest of who can most righteously claim to be fighting to defend seniors' rights to earned benefits. It will not matter whether any real threat exists. If we're really successful, someone will organize a protest on the Mall and the largest corporations will express solidarity with seniors in full-page ads in the Washington Post. The best-case scenario might be a host of amendments to SSBI that increase deficit spending.

I'm betting the so-called third rail of Social Security can be touched if we address the core concerns of its defenders. The name of the program is hard to improve upon; it is a simple expression of what just about anyone would want from a publicly funded safety net. That's why I have incorporated it in my SSBI moniker. But scratch the surface of the existing program (and we will do more than that in this chapter), and we find it's ripe for reform. Now might be the perfect time to consider reforms. Young people do not trust the system, anyway, and they're abandoning party politics in droves. The sooner we come clean about what can and cannot be promised, the better. When we finally admit that it's not a savings plan but a redistribution system, we can objectively examine alternative policies to determine who is paying whom, how and how much.

Social Security's demographic/fiscal problem is well known. Not so widely recognized is the significance of the fact that the associated entitlement is created by contributions. Each retiree's benefits are paid by taxes collected from several workers. This means those who would rather not "contribute" must be taxed to pay current beneficiaries. It also means that every tax dollar creates an entitlement to future benefits that will require several more people to pay the taxes that fund payment of those benefits.[37] Fiscally responsible changes are resisted by several generations of workers who were promised benefits based on taxes paid over a lifetime of work. They deserve what was promised. However, we need to stop this cycle of dependency by making no further promises. The only way out is to eliminate the tax.

---

[37] At the end of 2021, there were 56 million people receiving retirement benefits and 9 million receiving disability benefits; 179 million were paying OASDI taxes (US SSA 2022a: 2).

Responsible administration of an income security program must address solvency and the limit to what we can afford. Because SSBI includes younger people, roughly twice as many people will receive SSBI payments as currently receive OASDI alone. However, the SSBI entitlement is one year at a time; any individual can move in and out and up or down in the continuum of net payments, depending on their own fortunes. Since payments are tied to the income distribution, the total number and amount of payments are unlikely to change much. This means *SSBI, with approximately 100 million beneficiaries, would have only half as many dependents as Social Security, which has over 200 million contributors and beneficiaries* (Richardson 2013: 124).

Free to Work (FTW) and SSBI

SSBI is intended to solve two related problems: income inequality and insolvency of Social Security. The BIG may or may not gain acceptance, and in any event may take a decade or two to adopt, even with provisions that pay all benefits earned under the old program. Before we even begin serious consideration of entitlement reform alternatives, we should discontinue payroll taxes and tax expenditures to grant relief to US households with low and moderate incomes. By funding these obligations from income taxes, we can simultaneously improve the fiscal condition of Social Security and Medicare. I call this plan Free to Work because it lowers the marginal tax rate on wages and self-employment income. In addition to providing immediate relief for workers, it would freeze Social Security entitlements and put Social Security and Medicare on a fully funded pay-as-you-go basis.

In Table 5.1 below, the second column (labeled SQ) provides a baseline of relevant program features, revenue and cost. The third and fourth columns provide the same information for my proposals for comparison. As indicated in the third row under Funding Sources, a federal income (FI) surtax would supplement revenue from elimination of tax expenditures (TE), while the basic income (BI) surtax (row 4) would not apply until and unless we adopt the income guarantee. Detailed explanations of each proposal follow.

Table 5.1 Status Quo (SQ) entitlements vs. FTW and SSBI

	SQ	FTW	SSBI
Funding Sources			
Payroll tax	$1.314 trillion. Employee and employer each pay 7.65% of wages for OASDI and HI; high earners pay an additional 0.9% for HI.	Eliminated	Eliminated
Tax expenditures (TE)	$1.467 trillion (*forgone* revenue), including FTW items plus mortgage interest, state & local income and property taxes, capital gains, charitable contributions, employer contributions for medical insurance, and child credit.	+$915 billion. All deductions eliminated except pension contributions and earnings, individuals' health care expenditures, and the new child allowance, reducing forgone revenue to $552 billion.	+$1.215 trillion ($300 billion child allowance included in SSBI amount)
Federal Income tax (FI)	$2.044 trillion revenue. Seven tax brackets from 10% to 37%	+$849 billion. Itemized deductions eliminated; surtax of 5, 10, and 15% for incomes exceeding $50,000, $100,000, and $200,000 (and twice these amounts for married couples).	+$1.576 trillion. Negative tax applied at $15,000 (SSBI); surtax same as FTW except higher rates (10, 20, and 30%).
Basic Income (BI) surtax	N/A	N/A	Earned income is taxed at 25% and unearned income at 30% up to the SSBI amount ($15,000); affects net cost of SSBI already reflected in FI tax revenue.
Entitlements			
Age eligible	OASDI 62, HI 65	No change	18
Amount	$1.972 trillion. Includes OASDI benefit payments (average $15,000) and all Medicare costs	No change. OASDI same payments but fully taxable; Medicare same as SQ.	-$3.407 trillion. OASDI and HI same as FTW; SSBI ($15,000) adds $1.435 trillion to cost

	SQ	FTW	SSBI
Other cash entitlements	$301 billion (SSI, EITC, TANF, and SNAP)	+$61 billion. EITC replaced by the child allowance, which is accounted for in tax expenditures. SSI, TANF, and SNAP same as SQ.	+$301 billion (all four programs replaced by SSBI)
Net Costs			
	-$658 billion (OASDI and HI costs exceed FICA revenue.)	**-$147 billion** (Deficit reduced by 78 percent.)	**-$315 billion** (Includes legacy Social Security benefits of $405 billion)
Note: All revenue and cost estimates are for 2021; sources are the FY 2023 President's Budget (OMB 2023), Department of the Treasury (2023) estimate of tax expenditures, and Social Security and Medicare Trustees' reports (SSA 2022a and HHS 2022a).			

Paying for benefits no longer funded by the payroll tax will require raising other taxes. TE are an obvious target because 1) they increase inequality, 2) they are large enough to offset most payroll tax revenues, and 3) the TCJA made itemized deductions less valuable to lower income taxpayers.[38] It will not work to take on every special interest by arguing the merits of each item one at a time. A better approach is to repeal them all at once (Olson 1982: 236-7). There are two that affect a very large number of taxpayers and may be worth keeping. Tax fairness, in my view, demands elimination of special exemptions, including broad-based deductions from income (such as home mortgage interest) that favor the wealthy and encourage debt. However, I would retain deductions for retirement savings and health care expenditures because encouraging taxpayers' voluntary efforts to provide for their own income security will reduce reliance on the federal safety net.

We should be concerned about the limited oversight of tax expenditures; they continue to receive very little attention from Congress even as demand for evaluation of direct spending programs has increased (Harris, Steuerle, and Quakenbush 2018). Even though we know less about the effects of this type of spending on public outcomes, these programs – by design – bypass the annual budget process. While discretionary programs must receive annual appropriations, tax expenditures are permanent and increase automatically with taxpayers' personal and business spending decisions. Another cause for concern is the way we account for TE – as reductions in revenue, not increases in spending. This hides the true size of our government.

---

[38] For example, the impact of the popular home mortgage interest deduction is much lower due to the $750k limit and doubling of the standard deduction.

Even mandatory spending programs such as Social Security and Medicare are far more transparent about their current and future costs and benefits.

Many taxpayers count on TE to reduce their tax bill, and they benefit substantially. However, these taxpayers are relatively wealthy. It makes little sense to pursue a progressive reform agenda including the BIG while ignoring TE. The burden of funding government must fall on those able to bear the burden, and it is more equitable to distribute that burden evenly on a progressive scale than to skew it in favor of special interests. Insofar as we have any intention of actually paying for government, every dollar deducted from taxable income necessitates higher tax rates for others. It is unreasonable to ask the majority of taxpayers to shoulder tax increases while leaving intact deductions that apply to a small minority.

My own proposal is more ambitious than most, but others have called for reducing tax expenditures. Marr, Huang, and Friedman (2013), in an Obama era proposal to reform the tax code, noted support of the Debt Reduction Task Force for such measures because they provide the largest subsidies to those least in need of financial incentives (to buy a home, send a child to college, or save for retirement, to name just a few of the most popular deductions).

Exemption from income taxation of employer-paid health insurance premiums is the largest TE and it affects more taxpayers than any other. Employers treat premiums like wages, which are fully deductible as a business expense, yet these premiums are not taxable to the insured individuals. Because this policy disproportionately benefits higher income individuals (Gruber 2010, Burtless and Milusheva 2013), I propose to eliminate the expenditure, thereby making employer-paid premiums taxable. Due to the high standard deduction, lower income individuals may not see any increase in federal income tax liability; if they do, it will be offset by payroll tax savings. To equalize treatment of individuals with and without employer health plans, all health insurance premiums and out-of-pocket medical expenses would qualify as adjustments to gross income.[39] The rationale for retaining special treatment of medical expenses is that health care is essential – and it is high on the list of household expenses, especially for the poor. Just as it is good policy to encourage savings, we should provide incentives for preventive health care.

---

[39] Under current law, individuals' share of health insurance premiums for employer plans and self-employed individuals' premiums are not subject to FICA; they are treated as adjustments to gross income (not itemized). Participants in high-deductible plans can use Health Savings Accounts (HSAs) to exclude additional amounts from taxation. Other premiums and medical expenses are not deductible unless they exceed 10 percent of AGI.

As indicated in Table 5.1, FTW and SSBI would eliminate deductions for mortgage interest as well as state and local income and property taxes. These are significant deductions taken by millions of middle-class taxpayers. Removing them will be politically difficult, but both work against the goals of SSBI and therefore need to go. The mortgage deduction inflates property prices, encourages debt, and favors high income individuals and families. The deduction for state and local taxes subsidizes spending that adds to the high cost of living in wealthier areas. Capping them is one of the few good things in the TCJA; eliminating them would be even better. If these deductions remain, FI surtaxes will have to be even higher under FTW and SSBI.

Lower taxation of capital gains props up stock prices and reduces taxes on the wealthy. The market was soaring even before the TCJA, and as data in Chapter 2 indicate, other changes over the last half century have shifted tax burdens onto the working class. Retaining this benefit would make higher FI surtaxes necessary, and it would be unfair to taxpayers who do not own equities outside of retirement plans.

Charities and other non-profit organizations that rely on the charitable deduction to encourage higher donations will scream for an exception. However, if we are serious about helping the poor, we cannot justify funding middlemen selected by individual taxpayers. Eliminating this TE is not cutting assistance by the amount of the tax deductions; it's transferring targeted donations (charities) to universal donations (the BIG). Some organizations will struggle and many taxpayers will find it unpleasant to dig deeper or curtail charitable giving. But the status quo is inefficient and unfair compared to marginally increasing cash assistance to the needy. Keeping the deduction would require raising the FI surtax on everyone, not just those who give a lot of their income. It would also continue to subsidize activities that are neither charitable nor available to all, such as education and religious practices.

My analysis is "static;" it does not account for behavioral changes. SSBI reforms will certainly (and intentionally) increase deductions for retirement and health plan contributions, thereby reducing Federal Income Tax (FIT) revenue (Burman, Toder, and Geissler 2008). Not everyone will do so; some will pay debts and others will spend it all. On the other hand, employers will not spend all of their payroll tax savings on deductible expenses – meaning their taxable income will go up. However, it is highly unlikely that increased business taxes will offset reductions in individual taxes. TE reductions will redistribute roughly $1 trillion from special interests to (all) employers, workers, and small businesses, likely boosting consumption and stimulating tax revenue. But this is all speculation. Serious consideration of SSBI will require application of a sophisticated tax model that would improve upon my crude estimates and help address such complications. Even then, ideally, we would collect a few years of data and then incorporate the surtaxes in tax brackets and marginal tax rates to balance the budget.

Child care is another area that deserves exceptional treatment. I do not believe we should encourage or discourage having children. First of all, from the standpoint of human and ecological health, population growth may not be beneficial. Secondly, each couple and women in particular have the right to make reproductive decisions for themselves. Yet because the state has a vested interest in a larger tax base, tax incentives and other public services targeting children are motivated by more than just humanitarian concerns. Deficit finance has created an unhealthy reliance on continued growth, and there are serious challenges to slowing, stopping, and reversing this trend. There are risks either way, and we have to manage them. That means managing immigration, as well. Even with the citizenship requirement, SSBI will encourage immigration, so we will have to incorporate its effects. That is easier said than done, but I would not be writing this book if the strategy of avoiding difficult political choices worked. We need to strike the right balance between leaving parents completely alone and allowing people to shift the burden of their decisions onto society – and to help those raising our future generations without encouraging excess growth. At the same time, we can reverse the legacy of debt not just by shouldering the burden of care for the elderly, but by investing in young people.

A neutral, fair policy would treat children and their parents at least as well as others. We're not doing that now, because as discussed in Chapter 2, our social welfare programs are stingy and impose unreasonable work requirements. My bottom line on tax treatment of children is the purpose of a federal safety net, which is to help people emerge from and avoid falling into poverty. FTW would eliminate the child tax credit (or CTC, currently $2000) because it is insufficient for low-income households and unnecessary for those with high incomes. Instead, I propose a child allowance of $5000 per child, which is close to the estimated marginal cost of each additional family member in the Federal Poverty Guidelines (see Figure 5.2).[40] It would operate as a negative income tax (like the SSBI), meaning the benefit is reduced by income. The full amount is available up to household incomes approximately equal to the poverty guideline; thereafter, it is recovered by a surtax of 10 percent on income above those thresholds until the full amount is recovered. For example (and as illustrated in Table 5.3), a married couple with two children and income of $20,000

---

[40] This approach and amount are consistent with recommendations by Shaefer et al. (2018) "to reduce child poverty and income instability, and eliminate extreme poverty among families with children in the United States."

per year would receive the full $10,000 child allowance (FTW Tax column) because the threshold for their household is $30,000. The same family with an income of $40,000 would receive $9000 ($10,000-(0.1 X ($40k-$30k)); at $80,000, the benefit is $5000; at $130,000 and above, it is zero.

SSBI would incorporate the child allowance by adding it to the BIG amount. In other words, a single individual with one child would get $20,000 and a married couple with two children would get $40,000. The negative income tax would claw back the child care amounts at the same rate as the basic amount via the SSBI surtax (25 percent of earned income and 30 percent of unearned income). Extending the example from the preceding paragraph, this means a married couple with two children would receive no net SSBI benefit if their income exceeds $160,000. A couple with no children would reach the break-even point at $120,000.[41]

Parents make real contributions to society in raising the next generation. The child allowance makes it easier to do the work of caring for children without taking on extra jobs to obtain cash. It may help one parent stay home or work part-time, and/or help cover the cost of child care. The benefit of couples living together, with or without marriage, is obvious; each adult gets the SSBI amount, regardless.

Figure 5.2 Federal Poverty Guidelines

2023 POVERTY GUIDELINES FOR THE 48 CONTIGUOUS STATES AND THE DISTRICT OF COLUMBIA	
Persons in family/household	Poverty guideline
1	$14,580
2	$19,720
3	$24,860
4	$30,000
5	$35,140
6	$40,280
7	$45,420
8	$50,560
For families/households with more than 8 persons, add $5,140 for each additional person.	

Source: US HHS 2023

---

[41] In both cases, this applies to wage income only. A SSBI surtax of 30 percent would apply to unearned income.

What replaces Social Security? Obviously, we must satisfy existing obligations. However, grandfathering "earned" benefits will not satisfy everyone. In fact, the admission that we cannot increase annuities will provoke strong opposition by anyone heavily invested in the status quo. Many low-income workers who are 10-20 years from retirement have already paid a lot into Social Security, have no other savings or retirement plan, will spend any increase in take-home pay, and may find themselves in poverty when they are too old to work and the benefit earned decades earlier isn't enough to pay rent. We need to replace it with something.[42]

The new safety net should address a number of important questions: Why is our largest income support program based on attainment of an arbitrary retirement age? How can we justify taxing the poor to pay benefits to the rich? Not all old people are poor and not all poor people are old. We need to change the basis of payments from age to need. A lot can happen over a lifetime. A federal income support "safety net" should not withhold benefits people need today because we think they will need it years from now. Benefits should be available to any adult citizen who can demonstrate need based on income alone. Should the new safety net cover everyone below the poverty line, regardless of age or employment status? How much are we willing to spend? How will it be distributed? Who will pay for it? These questions will stoke fear and anger that more people will starve; others will be afraid of skyrocketing taxes. It's time we had the difficult conversation about goals and effectiveness of federal social welfare policy. We need to engage citizens in prioritizing federal spending (e.g., domestic vs. defense), defining the federal role (vs. state and local governments and the private sector), and considering everyone's needs (not just retirees). All these questions will be easier to address when we have increased the amount of information and the flexibility to use it by simplifying the tax structure.

How much help are we able and willing to provide? If we're too stingy, poverty persists. On the other hand, excess generosity invites moral hazard and bankrupts the system. A reasonable place to start is $1250/month, for two reasons: It is roughly where experts have established the poverty guideline and it is also near the average benefit level for the Social Security program we are replacing. Numbers will be crunched and the political process will yield a compromise of some sort. But

---

[42] I propose a broader safety net, but if we stick with retirees only, an option worth considering is to gradually transition to flat benefits (Biggs et al. 2016). Others prefer private sector (charity) or state/local government solutions (Tanner 2015: 2). As indicated later in this chapter, federal programs eliminated by SSBI may be replaced in some form by these entities. However, our experience with proposals to privatize Social Security suggests that route for reform is unlikely to succeed.

hopefully, we will not repeat the mistake of spending now and taxing or inflating later. Whatever is decided regarding eligibility rules and benefits, it should be obligated and paid for on budget, i.e., one fiscal year at a time. This rule provides flexibility to make adjustments as needed to the fiscal and political environments. It will work if the benefit remains universal, i.e., everyone remains in the same boat and factions are not allowed to throw others overboard or sink the ship, so to speak. In other words, we can revisit the benefit amounts, tax rates, and thresholds as needed according to performance of the US economy and income inequality trend data.

In the last 25 years, several other serious, comprehensive (national level) basic income proposals have surfaced in the US. In 1998, Garfinkel, Huang, and Naidich (2006) proposed a BIG to improve effectiveness of US federal poverty reduction programs, including Social Security. They analyzed four alternative plans targeting the elderly, adults, and children that would hold OASDI beneficiaries harmless (paying the guarantee or the retirement benefit, but not both) and finance payments by making BIG payments subject to FIT, eliminating personal exemptions from the FIT, offsetting OASDI payments, and eliminating 115 federal programs – including tax expenditures that favor high-income individuals and families. The most generous plan would pay each adult $6,000 and require raising income taxes by about 5 percent.

In 2006, Charles Murray (2016) presented an ambitious negative income tax version of BIG, "the Plan," to replace all national income support programs with a single annual payment. In 2016, he renamed it a "UBI grant" and made some minor revisions to reflect changes in the economic landscape such as the Affordable Care Act. Every American 21 or older would qualify for a $13,000 grant ($3000 of which is dedicated to health care) that would replace Social Security, Medicare/Medicaid, and all other "welfare" programs. He would pay for it with existing revenues plus savings from the programs eliminated and a graduated surtax of 10-30 percent on incomes of $30-60,000 to recoup up to half the guaranteed amount.

Alan Sheahen (2012, Ch. 13) proposed a $10,000 refundable tax credit for adults 18 or over who have been in the country for at least 5 years. This BIG would pay the tax credit or Social Security, whichever is greater. It would be financed by eliminating most "loopholes," the standard deduction, and personal exemptions from the FIT. It would also replace over 100 federal welfare programs and make significant cuts to the defense budget.[43]

---

[43] Sheahen also assumed Social Security would be phased into the BIG program. His financing options went beyond those needed to pay for the estimated costs of the proposed BIG – providing a menu of sorts that included raising FIT rates, eliminating all but "single" FIT filing

Andy Stern (2016: 201-15) proposed a UBI of $1000/mo. for adults 18-64 and for older people who do not receive at least that much in Social Security benefits. He would replace Social Security (in the long term) and reform the health care system with one that costs less and is not employer-based. In addition, to fund the expense of UBI, he suggested the following options: 1) eliminate many of the welfare programs (such as SNAP, housing assistance, and EITC); 2) eliminate most tax expenditures; 3) adopt a Value Added Tax (VAT) of 5-10 percent; 4) tax stock transactions (at 0.1-0.5 percent); 5) tax wealth (net worth), e.g., 1.5 percent on assets exceeding $1 million; and 6) trim the budget, especially military spending and subsidies to farms and oil and gas companies.

Andrew Yang's (2018) Freedom Dividend proposal for a UBI was the centerpiece of his campaign for President of the United States. The plan featured a $1000/month benefit for all US citizens 18 or over. Eligible beneficiaries could choose to keep their current benefits (welfare, food stamps, disability, etc.) or take the dividend, but they would not receive both. He would pay for this with a VAT of 10 percent, additional Social Security taxes on the wealthy (no cap), eliminating favorable income tax treatment of capital gains, and additional taxes on a financial transactions and carbon.

Economic Security Project co-founder Chris Hughes (2018: 91-4, 165-9) prefers a far less ambitious EITC-style benefit of $500/mo. for every *working* adult in a household with income less than $50,000/yr. (adjusted for the cost of living in each state). He would pay for it by raising taxes for those with incomes exceeding $250,000/yr. as follows: 1) taxing capital gains and dividends at the same rate as wage income, 2) capping deductions at 28 percent, 3) eliminating the exclusion of gains on inherited assets, and 4) raising the marginal tax rate to 50 percent. Although his scheme is limited to working people, he would include those not collecting paychecks but caring for dependents under 6 or over 70 and others who are enrolled in college.

The plan that most resembles my own was published by the New School a year after the first edition of this book (Zewde et al. 2021). Their Guaranteed Income plan does not touch Social Security; it expands the EITC beyond wage earners. Like SSBI, it utilizes a negative income tax approach and their presentation uses data visualizations to show people how the change will affect them according to their incomes. They also illustrate the plan's projected impact on racial income inequality. The benefit is at the poverty level ($12,500 per individual, with an additional $4500 per child) and phases out near the national median income.

---

status, a FIT surcharge on incomes over $1 million, eliminating the payroll tax cap, taxing stock trades, taxing wealth, raising the capital gains tax rate, and raising the estate tax rate.

What about SSBI? As discussed previously, it is universal and unconditional. In other words, it avoids social engineering requirements that add to the cost of administration and serve primarily to exclude people. It would replace all existing federal income support programs and it would not be adjusted for locality, marital status, dependents, or any other statistical criteria. Other institutions (e.g., state and local governments or charities) may adapt their programs to eliminate redundancies or to fill gaps in cash assistance or social services according to the needs, preferences, and means of their constituents.

SSBI has six goals: (1) honest accounting, (2) encourage work and entrepreneurship, (3) encourage savings, (4) simplify welfare policy, (5) minimize transition and implementation cost, and (6) promote equity.[44]

Honest accounting (Goal 1) is achieved by gradual elimination of unfunded liabilities for future benefit payments. My proposal honors existing obligations to pay earned benefits and makes no additional promises. It also eliminates the payroll tax and Trust Fund mechanism by paying benefits from general fund revenues enhanced by the aforementioned FI and BI surtaxes. The official US Federal Poverty Guidelines form the basis of the guarantee because they provide a fair estimate of need that anchors the program to its primary purpose of reducing poverty. The guidelines also help maintain a sustainable balance between SSBI payments and taxes, because they are adjusted each year to reflect macroeconomic conditions.

Work and savings incentives (Goals 2 and 3) are also improved under SSBI. The surtax transitioning from low to middle income provides a path to escape the poverty trap via work, because SSBI payments are only reduced by ¼ of the amount earned. The benefit is universal, so poor individuals and families no longer have to enter the maze of social services programs to find out which cash benefits they can get and what happens if they earn additional income. SSBI payments are determined one year at a time and the responsibility for saving shifts to workers. Those with low incomes are no longer forced to contribute their first 7.65 percent of earnings to fund others' benefits; they can put that same amount – perhaps supplemented by a portion of their SSBI payment – into savings they own and control. Entrepreneurs can save earnings that are not going toward Social Security or Medicare to start a small business and improve its chances of success. In addition, they have a safety net to protect them from the worst possible effects of misfortune or failure. They may be able to hire

---

[44] These six goals are based on recommendations of the Concord Coalition (2005), which identified several objectives of Social Security reform designed to ensure long-term fiscal sustainability, raise national savings, and improve generational equity.

help for slightly less and/or encourage them to stay by investing funds they previously submitted in payroll taxes in an employee retirement plan.

SSBI is just one step toward simplification of federal welfare policies (Goal 4). The simple formula of relatively generous cash payments with no eligibility requirements (except citizenship and age 18) removes the bureaucratic gate and puts decisions on ends and means in the hands of the recipient. SSBI will affect all other social programs. Each will serve beneficiaries with more cash in hand, and they will face pressure to improve targeting and effectiveness. Some programs will be able to better serve those with the greatest needs. State and local governments may find it easier to tailor their programs to supplement the SSBI than to build collages of benefits to satisfy requirements of smaller federal programs. Of course, some programs may no longer be needed at all.

SSBI is unavoidably complex and controversial, because it would significantly impact every American. However, I believe the actual transition can be less trouble than the deliberation process. Keeping it simple (Goal 5) would include a) using existing tax schedules and simple formulas to integrate SSBI payments and surtaxes, b) careful attention to achieve positive net impact on most individuals' cash flow, and c) designating familiar and reliable administrators (the Social Security Administration, or SSA, and the Internal Revenue Service, or IRS) to process funding, claims, and payments. My design work in this book is an example of (a) and (b).

Funding SSBI from income taxes instead of payroll taxes addresses equity issues – not just between rich and poor but also between old and young (Goal 6). Under the Federal Insurance Contributions Act (FICA), workers and employers pay for all benefits. In general, this means the young support the old. However, many older people – especially the poor – continue to work and pay taxes that fund benefit payments to people with larger, mostly unearned income. SSBI flips this around. Shifting from payroll tax to FIT funding spreads the burden to include those with unearned income, who tend to be older and enjoy higher incomes. Young workers who do not even earn enough to pay income taxes will no longer support retirees with higher incomes in exchange for a vanishing promise of future benefits. Poor young and middle-aged individuals will receive financial assistance. Those who earn higher incomes will pay no more than their elders with similar incomes.

The SSA will administer the program (using information shared by the IRS) because SSA's expertise is determining benefits and issuing payment to millions of beneficiaries. SSA will have to devise a system of estimating SSBI payments using recent tax returns and making (monthly) checks or automatic deposits on time. Not everyone will receive SSBI payments, because the guarantee is offset by a SSBI surtax on incomes above the guaranteed amount that exhausts the SSBI at a gross income of about five times the SSBI amount. Social Security benefits are also subject to income tax. Finally, there is a progressive federal income surtax that applies to most incomes exceeding $50,000.[45] Coordination with the IRS could minimize cash exchange using FIT withholding.

Estimated Impact on Federal Revenue and Spending

FTW and SSBI proposals to change the federal tax code are designed to shift the balance of power from capital to labor and thereby reverse increasing inequality of incomes in the US. The direction is clear but it is important to dig deeper and quantify the impact on revenues and expenditures. A neutral shift from the payroll tax to federal income taxes would maintain the equal burden distribution between individuals and employers. However, corporations pay just 15 percent of Federal Income Taxes (FIT)[46] and corporations' share of TE is just 8 percent (US Treasury 2023), so reforms will necessarily have the most impact on taxes paid by individuals. As indicated in Table 5.1, in 2021, TE were $1.467 trillion. FTW would eliminate all corporate TE and all but two individual TE: pension contributions and earnings ($225 billion) plus individuals' health care expenditures ($27 billion).[47] Eliminating the $2000 child credit would save $73 billion (plus $43 billion in outlays for refundable credits), but FTW would replace it with a $5000 child allowance that would cost about $300 billion. For simplicity's sake, the entire amount is treated as a tax expenditure

---

[45] The surtaxes apply all three recommendations for optimal tax policy by academic economists Peter Diamond and Emmanuel Saez (2011: 166) – high and rising marginal tax rates on very high earners, subsidy of low earnings phased out with high marginal tax rates, and significant taxation of capital income. And Thomas Piketty (2017: 660) says, "The evidence suggests that a rate on the order of 80 percent on incomes over $500,000 or $1 million a year not only would not reduce the growth of the US economy but would in fact distribute the fruits of growth more widely while imposing reasonable limits on economically useless (or even harmful) behavior."

[46] Table 2.1 in the FY 2023 President's Budget (US OMB 2023) shows, for 2021, estimated individual income tax receipts of $2.044 trillion and corporate income tax receipts of $372 billion.

[47] FY 2021 estimates (US Treasury 2023: Table 1, Estimates of Total Income Tax Expenditures for Fiscal Years 2021-2031). The pension figure includes defined benefit and defined contribution employer plans, IRAs, savers' credits, and self-employed plans (#140-44). The health care figure includes self-employed premiums, HSAs, and deductible medical expenses (#123-25). Seven items to be eliminated account for almost half of the total deductions and credits for individuals: #55 mortgage interest $29 billion, #59 net imputed rental income $124 billion, #68 capital gains $102 billion, #70 step-up basis of capital gains at death $42 billion, #117 charitable contributions $52 billion, #122 employer contributions for medical insurance $221 billion, and #156 social security benefits $27 billion.

in the table. This brings the FTW total TE to $552 billion, and the net revenue to $915 billion per year. An additional $61 billion would be saved by eliminating the Earned Income Tax Credit, which also has a TE component but is mostly refundable and therefore included as an entitlement outlay in the table.

FTW will need more than this to fully fund Social Security and Medicare payments, which were estimated at $1.972 trillion for 2021 – $1.133 trillion and $839 billion, respectively (US SSA 2022a, US HHS 2022a). All but **$147 billion** of the gap would be closed with an FI surtax on incomes that starts at 5 percent and rises to 10 percent and 15 percent at income levels well above the poverty level ($50,000, $100,000, and $200,000, respectively, for single filers and twice these amounts for married couples), which would increase income tax revenue by about $849 billion.[48] This improves upon the status quo (**$658 billion** deficit) by about $511 billion annually.

SSBI is a negative income tax coupled with two surtaxes. The first one is a flat surtax on incomes above the guaranteed amount (SSBI) – 25 percent on wages and 30 percent on unearned income – designed to maintain incentives to work while recovering the benefit at incomes about five times the poverty level basic income. The SSBI surtax determines net payments by subtracting FIT liability from the basic income amount; they are estimated at $1.435 trillion annually. The FI surtax under SSBI is the same as the FTW version, except rates are higher – 10, 20, and 30 percent (vs. 5, 10, and 15 percent). This surtax raises an estimated $1.698 trillion that more than covers the payments. This is offset, though, by eliminating about $122 billion in FIT that was being collected from people who would instead receive SSBI payments.

The net impact on federal revenue under SSBI, then, is $1.576 trillion annually.[49] It will replace direct transfers such as Supplemental Security Income (SSI), Earned Income Tax Credit (EITC), Temporary Assistance to Needy Families (TANF), and

---

[48] Surtax calculations use columns AG, AS, and BE in IRS Table 1.2 (US Treasury 2020a) for single filers and column U for married filers.

[49] These estimates use data in Tables 5.2 and 5.3 of payments to individuals and married couples at various income levels and IRS data on the number of filers of each type and income level (US Treasury 2020a). Surtax calculations use columns AG, AS, and BE in the IRS Table 1.2 for single filers and column U for married filers. Lost revenue calculations use columns AK, AW, and BI for single filers and column Y for married filers. Not included in this estimate is the number of citizens 18 or over who did not file returns because they did not have enough income. One source indicates there are roughly 15 million individuals and families in this category (Hodge 2005). Under SSBI, we can expect virtually all of them to file in order to obtain payments. Some have no income at all, while others may have earnings and/or Social Security payments very close to the SSBI amount. Without knowing the income distribution of this group, it is not possible to estimate their combined SSBI payments. However, it is almost certainly tens of billions of dollars annually, and possibly enough to warrant adjusting the FI surtax schedule.

Supplemental Nutrition Assistance Program (SNAP) payments that amounted to an estimated $301 billion in 2021.[50] With revenues of $1.215 trillion from reduced tax expenditures, $1.576 trillion from the FI surtax, and $301 billion from replacing other cash benefit programs and costs of $1.972 trillion in Social Security and Medicare benefits plus $1.435 trillion in SSBI payments, SSBI will have an initial deficit of **$315 billion**.

However, we need to consider that over time the amounts paid to retirees with higher incomes will disappear. The initial cost we just calculated (SS plus SSBI benefits) will slowly decrease as we transition to a steady state cost (SSBI benefits only) in which Social Security payments to taxpayers who would not qualify for SSBI payments disappear. This (legacy benefit) amount, which includes virtually everyone

---

[50] Itemized estimates are provided with descriptions of each program that follow; source is the FY 2023 President's Budget Historical Table 8.5, Outlays for Mandatory and Related Programs (US OMB 2023).

SSI is a federal means-tested program funded by general revenue of the US Treasury. It is designed to provide a monthly payment to aged, blind, or disabled people with limited income and resources. Adults, as well as children, can receive payments based on disability or blindness. In 2018, the average monthly federal payment was $568; payments were made to 7.7 million individuals (US SSA 2022c). Total federal outlays in 2021 were about $53 billion.

EITC is a refundable credit against federal income tax on earnings for those with relatively low incomes. If the credit reduces tax liability to zero, the government pays the amount left over as an income supplement. In 2022, qualifying income ceilings ranged from $16,480 for single filers with no children to $59,187 for married filers with three or more children. Credits ranged from $2 to $6935 (US Treasury 2022b). Total federal outlays in 2021 were about $61 billion (US OMB 2023).

The TANF program is designed to help needy families achieve self-sufficiency. States receive block grants to design and operate programs that accomplish one of the four purposes of the TANF program (US HHS 2022b):
- Provide assistance to needy families so that children can be cared for in their own homes
- Reduce the dependency of needy parents by promoting job preparation, work and marriage
- Prevent and reduce the incidence of out-of-wedlock pregnancies
- Encourage the formation and maintenance of two-parent families

Total federal outlays in 2021 for this and other family support assistance were about $25 billion (US OMB 2023).

SNAP (formerly known as the food stamp program) – the largest program in the domestic hunger safety net – offers nutrition assistance to millions of eligible, low-income individuals and families through a network of state agencies, nutrition educators, and neighborhood and faith-based organizations (USDA 2023). Total federal outlays in 2021 for this and other food and nutrition assistance programs were about $162 billion (US OMB 2023).

with gross incomes above \$50,000, is \$405 billion.[51] It is worth noting that legacy Social Security payments exceed SSBI payments even though many more people (almost 100 million) will receive payments under SSBI.[52] This is because many individuals and families with higher incomes receive Social Security payments two and even three times the SSBI amount.

Estimated Impact on Individuals

Funding Social Security and Medicare from general revenue instead of the payroll tax has at least three significant benefits:

1. It would remove the disincentive to start a business or to hire or retain individual employees represented by the combined 15.3 percent tax on labor.
2. Savings to small businessmen and any portion passed on to workers by employers improves their chances of entering or staying in the labor force.
3. Funding benefit payments by income taxes shifts the burden from the working poor to higher income households.

Employers' net income will increase; they save about \$650 billion per year in payroll taxes while giving up just \$100 billion in tax breaks. Aggregate impact on individuals is negative; their share of TE eliminated under FTW or SSBI is \$800 billion – about \$150 billion more than employees' share of payroll taxes. Many with high incomes who have become accustomed to low federal income taxes will be hit hard. Nevertheless, we should have no qualms about reversing policies that have worsened income inequality. FTW and SSBI correct past wrongs by shifting tax burdens to those able to bear them; leaving tax breaks in place will require raising taxes even more for people who have not enjoyed those breaks, which would be most unfair.

Generally, the poor will strongly favor my proposals while the rich will just as strongly oppose them – and of course, the poor outnumber the rich. But that does not justify the change, because might doesn't make right, whether it's measured by heads or dollars; that's why I wrote four chapters of moral justification. At some point, though, it becomes a political question: What's in it for me? I could conduct

---

[51] There are far too many variables to bother with projections, but if income distributions and tax rates remained stable, the SSBI surtax might be reduced along with legacy SS payments. SSBI payments at this steady state level would be covered with a surtax about 25 percent lower than the initial levy.

[52] Legacy SS benefits (paid to all filers with incomes exceeding \$50k) are estimated using IRS Table 1.4 (US Treasury 2020b). The number of individuals and families who will receive SSBI payments is estimated in the preceding paragraph; SS program beneficiaries total 65 million (US SSA 2022a: 2). Many people will receive both types of payments.

focus group interviews to illustrate how differently people in these groups live and think about money, but it would probably be more of a distraction than a source of insight. My operating assumption is that most poor people will take help where they can get it and most rich people believe they already pay too much in taxes. Those who need convincing that this is a move in the right direction are in the middle class; they, too, are most interested in how tax reforms will affect their own pocketbooks.

Detailed comparative static analysis (using IRS data for 2020) demonstrates that although the poor will have slightly higher incomes under FTW and much higher incomes under SSBI, helping them will not impose an unreasonable burden on others. As indicated in Figures 5.5a, 5.5b, 5.6a, and 5.6b, overall tax rates for wage earners and self-employed taxpayers under FTW and SSBI are lower than under the status quo (SQ) except at very high incomes ($160,000 for single filers and $320,000 for married filers). Those with unearned income would only pay more taxes if their annual income exceeds about $75,000 for single filers and $160,000 for married filers (see Figures 5.5c and 5.6c). At the high end ($160,000 and $320,000, respectively), their tax bills rise by 3-4 percentage points under FTW and 7 percentage points under SSBI. However, as shown in Figures 5.3a and 5.4a, this merely erases the advantage they currently enjoy over wage earners and the self-employed.

Under FTW, almost everyone above the Federal Poverty Guidelines – currently $14,580 for individuals and $30,000 for a family of four (US HHS 2023) – will have to pay more income tax, but most low and middle income taxpayers will be significantly better off (5-10 percent more net income) because their paychecks are at least 7.65 percent larger (see Tables 5.2 and 5.3). Benefits are significantly greater for low to middle income households under SSBI.

There is one exception – those receiving above average Social Security (OASDI) payments (e.g., $40,000 for singles or $80,000 for married couples). If this is their only source of income, they may not pay any federal income tax under SQ; under FTW, OASDI payments are fully taxable, so they would pay the same as others with similar incomes from earnings or investments – up to 8 percent of adjusted gross income. Under SSBI, they are significantly better off than with FTW or SQ. This group, having worked hard enough and long enough to pay significant sums into the system and finding themselves completely dependent on it, may be outraged by having their benefits taxed.[53] But their benefits are being paid by current taxes on

---

[53] While many are completely dependent on Social Security, those receiving the largest payments are most likely to have other sources of earned or unearned income. The table and figures provided do not mix sources.

others, and only a small fraction of benefits can be traced to previously taxed contributions.[54] Honestly, they fall into the same category as those who have become dependent on TE.

I'm sympathetic toward those who did not ask for special treatment and merely played by the established rules. On the other hand, I think we owe more to those who have carried disproportionate burdens. Other losers under SSBI will have similar stories (i.e., some variation of the Social Security example – loss of a deduction or exemption) or they will suffer indirectly due to spending reductions by others (federal, state, or local governments, charitable organizations, patrons whose taxes went up, etc.). Some will surely manage to persuade powerful Members of Congress to fight this change. But allowing exceptions to drive the debate could abort overdue reforms and impose tremendous opportunity costs on the undeserving middle class. Let's look at two examples of what FTW and SSBI would mean for a middle-income family and for a single, self-employed individual with higher earnings.[55]

Payroll taxes for the Smiths, a married couple with two children and combined wages of $75,000, which is slightly above the median household income (US Census Bureau 2022a), would be $5738. They take the standard deduction of $25,100 and purchase health insurance through the Affordable Care Act exchange.[56] Their SQ taxable income is $49,900 and 2021 FIT is $1607 (after deducting $4000 for the child tax credit. Their federal tax total is $5738 + $1607 = $7345 and their net disposable income is $63,555 after paying for health insurance ($4100).

Under FTW, their total tax bill (including the FTW child allowance of $10,000 per child) is just $90 and their disposable income is $70,810, which is $7255 or 11 percent higher. Since their earned Social Security benefits are frozen and the earnings that would have gone toward payroll taxes are available, they should consider investing some of those savings in an IRA or 401(k). Suppose they have IRAs and decide to invest $6000 ($3000 each). Their taxable income drops to $45,900; they get a tax refund of $630 and their disposable income is $65,540, which is still higher than the status quo (SQ) amount. Moreover, their net worth is $6000 higher and they have an asset they control. Will the Smiths actually save almost all of the increase in their disposable income for retirement? Not likely, but the point is that SSBI gives them plenty of options and far more financial security.

---

[54] "Actuarially, previously taxed contributions generally do not exceed 15 percent of benefits, even for retirees receiving the highest levels of benefits." (US Treasury 2023: 20).
[55] These calculations use the same assumptions, sources, and Excel formulas that produced results discussed in the next section and presented in Tables 5.2 and 5.3.
[56] See note 1 in Table 5.3.

Under SSBI, their taxable income would be the same as the FTW amount, but instead of paying taxes, they receive a SSBI payment of $16,152, which even after covering their health insurance cost *raises* their disposable income to $87,052, which is *higher than their combined wages and $23,497 (37 percent) higher than the status quo.*

Ms. Jones is a single, self-employed woman making $120,000 net profit annually, with itemized deductions of $20,000 for mortgage interest, $5,000 for charitable deductions, and the maximum $10,000 for state and local income and property taxes. She pays $7700 annually for health insurance. Her self-employment tax (OASDI + HI) liability (15.3 percent) is $17,182 and FIT is $12,755, which yields a net disposable income of $82,364.[57] Under FTW, the self-employment tax disappears, but so do itemized deductions. Now taking the standard deduction of $12,550, her taxable income is much higher, but her total tax bill is much lower ($20,449), and her disposable income is $91,852 – $9488 (12 percent) higher than under SQ. That's money she can reinvest in her business, spend, or save.

Under SSBI, her tax is slightly higher ($22,936), and her disposable income is $89,364, which is still $7000 (8 percent) higher than the SQ amount, *despite the 10 percent surtax on taxable income above $50,000.* Since $120,000 is a very nice income, especially for a single person, it may be surprising that Ms. Jones' take-home pay would be so much higher after losing over $20,000 in deductions, paying back all of the SSBI amount, and covering a FI surtax of 10 percent on taxable income above $50,000. Look at the numbers. She can pay her share of the FI surtax and have money left over because she no longer has to pay self-employment tax.

These hypothetical scenarios illustrate that for ordinary tax situations, under FTW and SSBI effective tax rates are much lower for workers – especially those who are self-employed – at all income levels. Naturally, taxpayers' experiences will vary and as stated earlier, those especially dependent on existing tax expenditures would have difficult adjustments to make under SSBI. People with mostly unearned and/or Social Security income will pay slightly more in taxes unless they have very high incomes, in which case the differences are more significant. For example, singles with ordinary unearned income (e.g., pensions or interest) of $500,000 and couples with unearned income of $1,000,000 would see their average tax rates rise from 28 or 29 percent to 50 percent, raising their tax bills by $112,000 and $212,000, respectively. This is a lot of money, but they were already paying six figure tax bills.

---

[57] To maintain comparability with those taking the standard deduction, items like mortgage interest and state taxes are not subtracted from disposable income, whereas (per the preceding Smith example), out-of-pocket health costs are subtracted.

An extreme case is the rich person or couple with 100 percent capital gains income. While they pay just 20 percent federal tax under SQ, they would be subject to ordinary income tax rates under FTW or SSBI. Their average tax rates would rise to the same 50 percent, but the increase would more than double their tax bills. In addition, my calculations of SQ taxes do not account for large tax deductions that may apply, in which case they could be paying an average rate below 20 percent and therefore face even larger increases under FTW and SSBI. There is no denying these are large sums, even for millionaires. My response to the outrage sure to come from this group is:

1. This is not restitution but cessation of indefensible redistributions from the working poor to the wealthy;

2. High marginal tax rates on upper incomes (up to 67 percent) merely restore the more equitable balance between taxation of labor and capital that allowed the working class to prosper in the US prior to 1980 (Tax Policy Center 2017b);[58] and

3. These policies will strengthen incentives to work by reducing marginal taxes on wages for those with low and middle incomes, thereby addressing the chronic reduction in labor force participation that acts as a brake on our economy.

To illustrate the distributional effects, I calculated the impact of FTW and SSBI on net incomes of single and married filers with five levels ($10k, 20k, 40k, 80k, and $160k for single filers and twice the amounts for married filers) and four types of income (wages; Schedule C or self-employment; OASDI or Social Security; and unearned income such as dividends, interest, or capital gains). All examples include estimated health insurance premium payments and standard or itemized deductions based on recent national averages from reliable sources. For married filers, I assumed two children and included the EITC and proposed child allowance. Then I calculated taxable income, taxes (including FICA for SQ), and net incomes under all three scenarios. Finally, I compared net incomes and average tax rates (total federal taxes as a percentage of gross income, including employer-paid health insurance premiums). Results for each income type at each level are shown in Tables 5.2 and 5.3.[59]

---

[58] See also Figure 2.1, which shows how dramatically fortunes shifted between upper and lower income groups around 1980, and Figure 3.2, which shows that current tax policies impose marginal tax rates above 60 percent on people barely above the Federal Poverty Guidelines while those with incomes several times as high experience marginal tax rates closer to 40 percent.

[59] High incomes where Social Security (OASDI) payments would reach a maximum assume the rest is unearned. For the sake of simplicity, none of the OASDI results are shown in the charts.

The most interesting results are in the last three columns, which compare tax rates for individuals and families with different *sources of income* and tax rates for individuals and families at different *levels of income*. Together, these data show how FTW and SSBI change relative taxation of wage, self-employment, and unearned income and how both reforms also change the slope or progressivity of tax rates at different levels of income, as compared to SQ. Figures 5.3 and 5.4 plot data from Tables 5.2 and 5.3 for those filing single tax returns and then for married couples filing jointly, holding the tax regime constant while varying types of income. Figures 5.5 and 5.6 plot the same data but hold income types constant while varying tax regimes.

In Figures 5.3a and 5.4a, which focus on SQ rates, we see first of all that at all but the lowest income levels, tax rates are lowest for those with unearned income and highest for the self-employed. For single filers, the difference is 10 percentage points at the low end ($10k), where those with unearned income pay zero taxes; at $160k, the average rates are 18 percent and 25 percent, respectively. At $20k, married wage earners with children, get EITC and CTC refundable credits of 25 percent at while those with unearned income only get the child tax credit of 14 percent. At the high end ($320k), wage earners and the self-employed pay 23 percent, while those with unearned income pay 17 percent. Clearly, this is the payroll tax effect. This is a best-case scenario in terms of inequality because the unearned estimates assume ordinary income tax rates, not the lower capital gains rates.

Figures 5.3b and 5.4b show tax rates for the same income types and levels under FTW. It's a very different picture, with rates starting at zero for single filers with all types of income and rising steadily to 21-23 percent. The impact of FTW is dramatic; it reduces taxes for everyone at lower levels of income and lowers tax rates for wage earners and the self-employed at incomes up to 6-8 times the basic income levels, thereby creating a truly progressive federal income tax. Due to taxation of employer paid health insurance, wage earners pay higher rates, but never more than three percentage points higher than the self-employed and unearned income groups, which pay the same rates at every level of income. Again because of the EITC and child allowance, the profile is more progressive for married filers, with a negative 50 percent rate at the low end. Average rates for all income types are within four percentage points (vs. a 12-point maximum spread under SQ), with wage earners paying slightly more, and they reach 21-23 percent for top level ($320k) incomes.

Figures 5.3c and 5.4c compare tax rates for the three income types under SSBI. The most significant change is at the low end ($10k), where (single filer) incomes more than double due to the generous SSBI negative income tax (-125 percent for wages and Schedule C and -120 percent for unearned incomes). Average rates stay close (within five percentage points), but in this case they are higher for unearned incomes until about $60k, where rates for wage incomes go higher (due to taxing employer paid health insurance premiums). At $160k, average rates are 25 percent for self-employed and unearned incomes and 28 percent for wage earners. For married couples, the child allowance drives the average rate at $20k down to -175 percent for wage and Schedule C incomes. Unearned income rates stay within five percentage points of the others and dip below wage rates at about $75k; at $320k, unearned and Schedule C rates are 24 percent and wage rates are 27 percent.

Now let's look at how the three tax schemes compare for each income type. While the first set of charts emphasized differences in taxation of income types under each individual tax scheme, the second set of charts compare tax rates between the three schemes for each income type. Figures 5.5a and 5.6a, which plot average tax rates for wage income, show that low- and middle-income wage earners pay much lower rates under FTW and SSBI. For example, a single person with wage income of $20,000 pays 11 percent under SQ, 4 percent under FTW, and gets a 46 percent payment ($9255) under SSBI. A married couple with $80,000 gross income and two children pays 9 percent under SQ but only 5 percent under FTW and receives a 13 percent payment ($12,586) under SSBI. Average tax rates for single and married filers are 15-16 percent at incomes of $80k and $160k, respectively, under FTW and SSBI, compared to 19 percent and 17 percent, respectively, for the SQ. At the top end ($160k and $320k), SQ and FTW rates are 23-24 percent, while SSBI rates climb to 27-28 percent.

Five percentage point tax increases do not seem like enough to pay for the huge increases in lower incomes. There are a couple of simple explanations. First of all, one percentage point applied to $320,000 is 32 percentage points for someone earning $10,000. Second of all, the highest FI surtaxes do not even affect incomes shown on these charts; they kick in at $200k and $400k for single and married filers, respectively. Under SSBI, single and married wage earners with incomes of $250k and $500k, respectively, will pay 38 percent of their adjusted gross income in taxes; those with unearned incomes of $500k and $1 million will pay 50 percent. These rates compare to 27-29 percent under SQ (at both levels), meaning very high-income households with ordinary deductions will face tax increases amounting to tens of thousands and even hundreds of thousands of dollars. Those currently enjoying tax breaks that will be eliminated to keep overall rates at this level will see even greater tax increases. There aren't many of them, but extra taxes on one multimillionaire can cover dozens of basic income payments.

Figures 5.5b and 5.6b compare rates for self-employed (Schedule C) income. The picture is very similar to the wage examples, except the spread is much larger due to the self-employment tax, especially at lower incomes. A single person with income of $20k pays 17 percent under SQ, which drops to 4 percent under FTW and -46 percent under SSBI. A married couple with an income of $80,000 and two children pays 15 percent under SQ, 1 percent under FTW, and -17 percent under SSBI. At the high end, rates range from 21 to 25 percent, with SSBI rates equal to or 1 percentage point higher than SQ and four points higher than FTW.

Figures 5.5c and 5.6c depict rates for those with unearned income. By design, rates don't change much at the low end because FTW and SSBI are meant to provide tax relief to workers and small business owners. Therefore, rates average 4 percent for single filers at $20k under SQ and FTW; under SSBI the same person would enjoy a tax rate of -41 percent. A married couple with income of $80,000 and two children would pay 3 percent under SQ, 1 percent under FTW, and -12 percent under SSBI. For singles at $160k, average rates are just 18 percent under SQ but rise to 21 percent under FTW and 25 percent under SSBI. For a married couple with two children and an income of $320k, rates are 17 percent under SQ, 21 percent under FTW, and 24 percent under SSBI. These (high end) rates are the same as for self-employed income and lower than for wage income.

Rates diverge much more for higher unearned incomes than for the other types. The gap is larger for unearned income (7 percent vs. 3-4) because SQ favors unearned income to such a degree – an inequality FTW and SSBI are designed to rectify. As shown in Figure 5.4a, the SQ rate for both wage and self-employed income at this level is 23 percent vs. 17 percent for unearned income. The gap would be even larger if we were to take into consideration extraordinary deductions such as reduced rates on capital gains that apply to unearned income.

Analysis of Treasury data demonstrates that it is feasible to relieve America's workers of the tremendous burden imposed by FICA taxes on their wages and self-employment earnings. The big tradeoffs in FTW are: 1) Individuals who have relied upon special tax benefits will lose them, and 2) All workers will have to save for retirement. These are controversial changes, but that's unavoidable for significant changes to the tax code or to Social Security. The case for eliminating the payroll tax is very strong. Nevertheless, it will encounter fierce resistance fueled by momentum and tradition. Once we recognize the need for change, I see no alternative to funding existing obligations for Medicare and Social Security that does not involve slashing tax expenditures. The numbers are too big and we cannot justify raising taxes on the middle class to continue special treatment of the wealthy.

Our economy will not crumble if capital gains and mortgage interest payments are fully taxable. In fact, it may restore some semblance of reality – and justice – to markets. This is not socialism; it's real capitalism, in which borrowers pay savers (instead of financial institutions that enjoy rents created by artificially low interest loans from a central bank). In other words, these two tradeoffs are not separate but related. Real interest rates must rise to encourage savings so that workers can obtain financial security during their working years as well as for retirement. They have been abandoned by employers who no longer find it profitable to fund pension benefits and by a government that has also made promises it can no longer keep. The mechanism and tax incentives are in place for privately funded savings accounts; unfortunately, wages are insufficient and yields are at the mercy of Wall Street, which is not a friend to Main Street, never mind workers. Until we figure out what can be done about monetary policy, the least we can do is use fiscal policy to mitigate the damage. Shifting the tax burden back to those with incomes that can bear the burden, through simple yet radical reforms along the lines of FTW and SSBI, is a blunt instrument to counter the blunt instrument of inflation that is pounding the working class even without help from regressive taxation.

My proposals offer no magic bullet. With or without adopting any part of them, we will eventually have to abandon the fantasy that our social insurance system will become solvent and wages will rise without any painful confrontations, choices, and uncertainties. The good news is that we have more room to maneuver than we may have thought.

Figure 5.3 SQ, FTW, and SSBI taxation of wages, Schedule C, and unearned incomes for *single* taxpayers

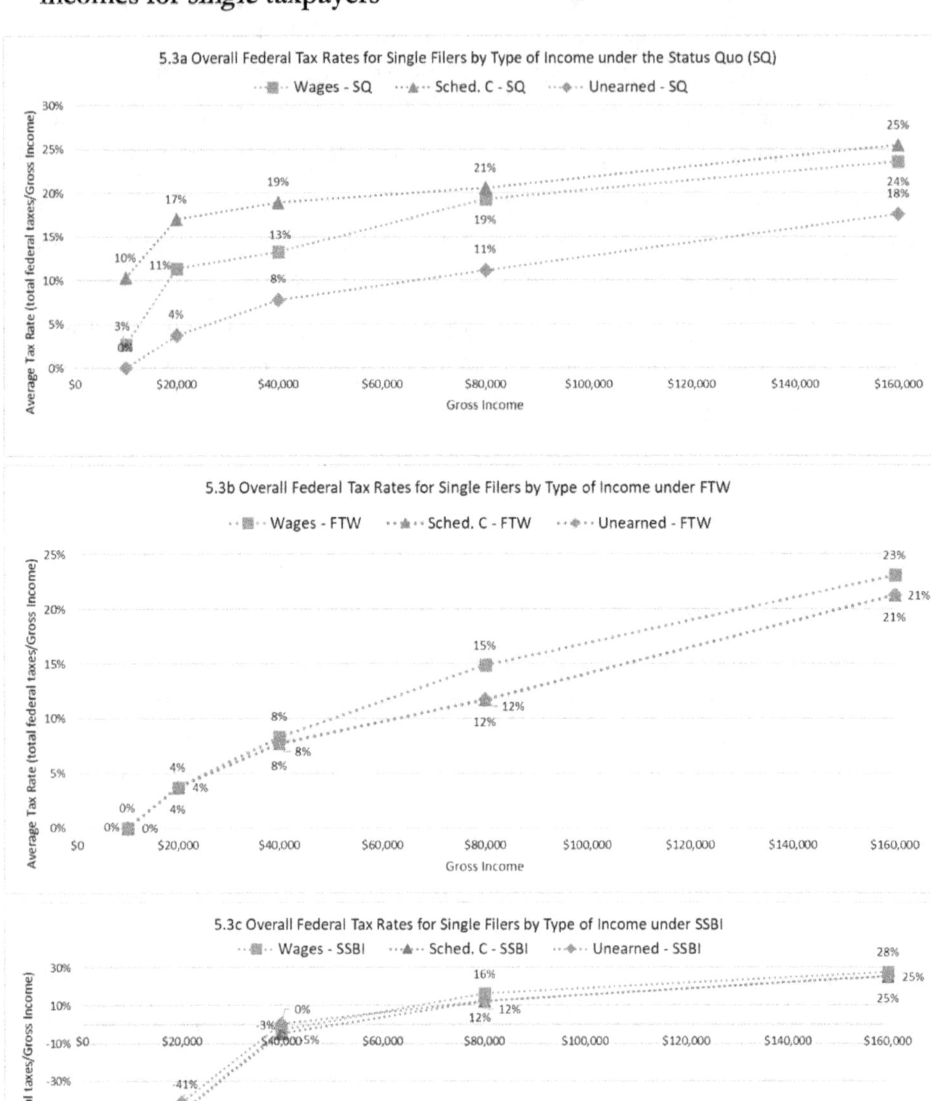

Figure 5.4 SQ, FTW, and SSBI taxation of wages, Schedule C, and unearned incomes for *married* taxpayers – including child allowance for two children

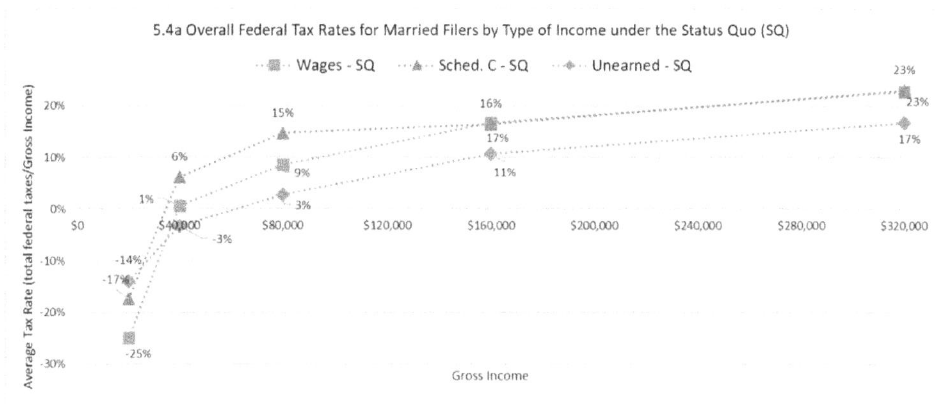

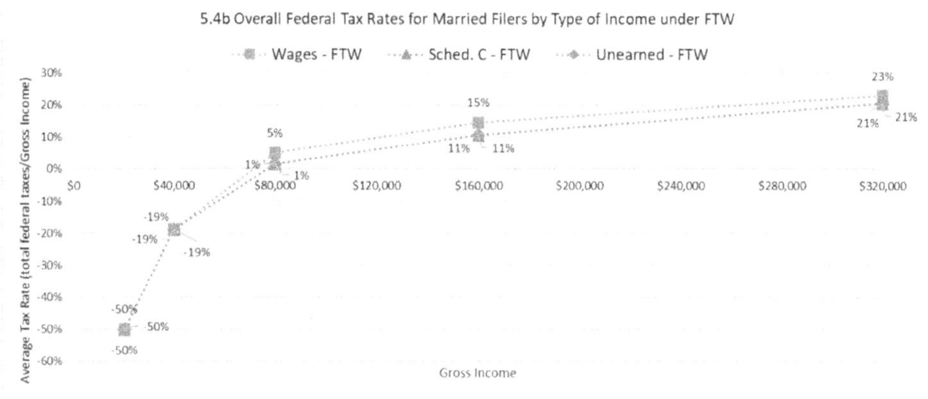

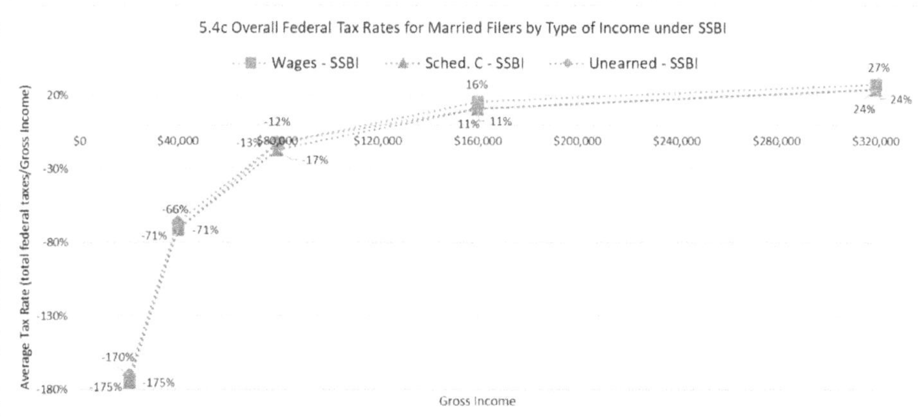

Figure 5.5 Wage, Schedule C, and unearned income taxation under SQ, FTW, and SSBI for *single* taxpayers

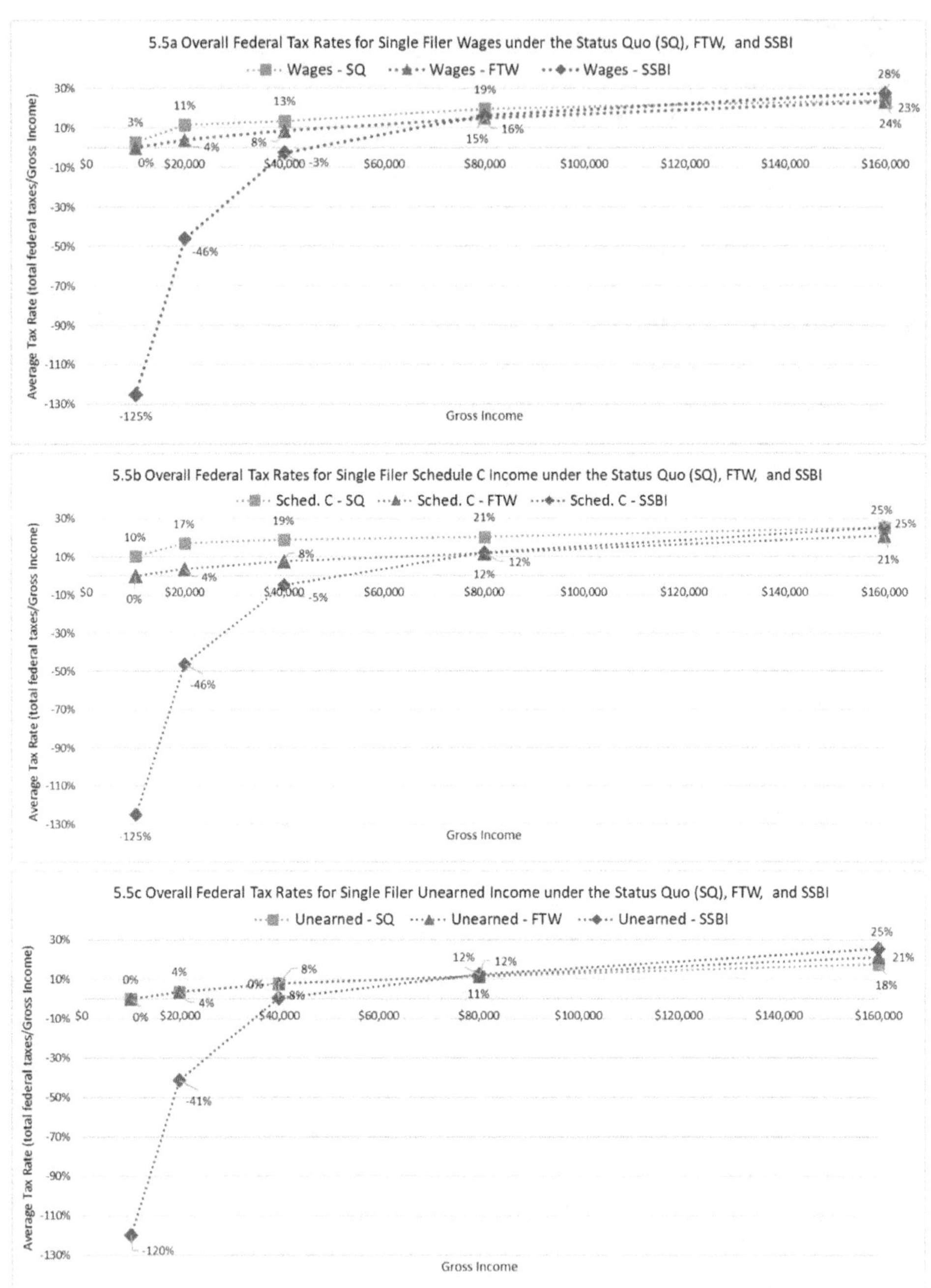

Figure 5.6 Wage, Schedule C, and unearned income taxation under SQ, FTW, and SSBI for *married* taxpayers – including child allowance for two children

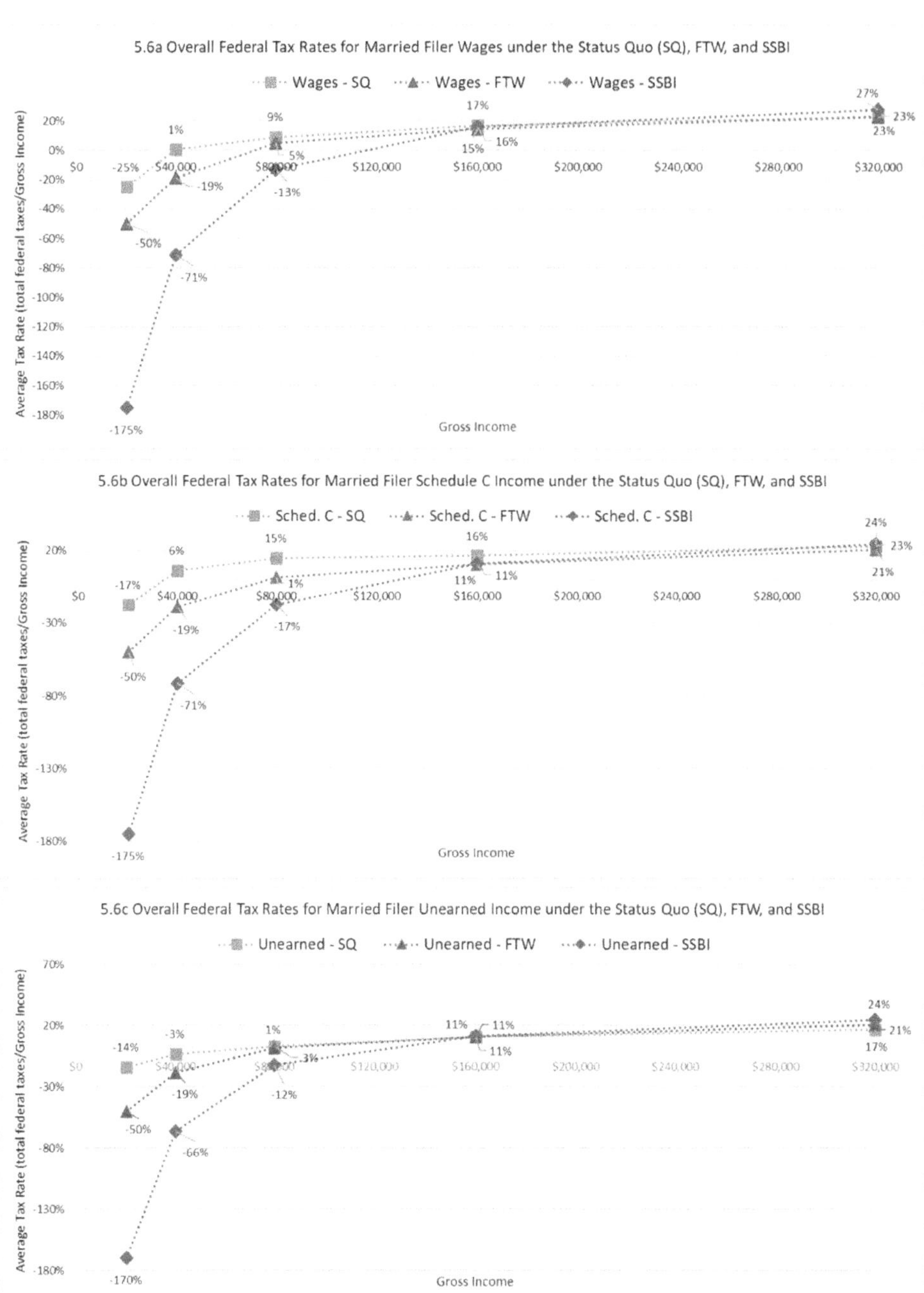

Table 5.2 Net income and overall federal tax rates for single filers by income type and amount under SQ, FTW, and SSBI

	Wages	Sched. C	OASDI	Unearned	Employer Health Premium 1/	Individual Health Premium 1/	Gross Income (incl. Emp. Health)	SQ Itemized 2/	SQ Taxable 1/3/	SQ FIT	FICA 3/	SQ EITC	SQ Net	FTW Taxable 1/3/4	FTW Tax	FTW Net	FTW Net – SQ Net	SSBI Taxable 1/3/	SSBI Tax	SSBI Net	SSBI Net – SQ Net	SQ Tax Rate	FTW Tax Rate	SSBI Tax Rate
1	10,000	0	0	0	0	0	10,000	0	0	0	765	498	9,733	0	0	10,000	267	0	-12,500	22,500	12,767	0.03	0.00	-1.25
2	0	10,000	0	0	0	0	10,000	0	0	0	1,530	498	8,968	0	0	10,000	1,032	0	-12,500	22,500	13,532	0.10	0.00	-1.25
3	0	0	10,000	0	0	0	10,000	0	0	0	0	0	10,000	0	0	10,000	0	0	-12,500	22,500	12,500	0.00	0.00	-1.25
4	0	0	0	10,000	0	0	10,000	0	0	0	0	0	10,000	0	0	10,000	0	0	-12,000	22,000	12,000	0.00	0.00	-1.20
5	20,000	0	0	0	0	0	20,000	0	7,450	745	1,530	0	17,725	7,450	745	19,255	1,530	7,450	-9,255	29,255	11,530	0.11	0.04	-0.46
6	0	20,000	0	0	0	0	20,000	0	3,450	345	3,060	0	16,595	7,450	745	19,255	2,660	7,450	-9,255	29,255	12,660	0.17	0.04	-0.46
7	0	0	20,000	0	0	0	20,000	0	0	0	0	0	20,000	7,450	745	19,255	-745	7,450	-9,255	29,255	9,255	0.00	0.04	-0.46
8	0	0	0	20,000	0	0	20,000	0	7,450	745	0	0	19,255	7,450	745	19,255	0	7,450	-8,255	28,255	9,000	0.04	0.04	-0.41
9	40,000	0	0	0	6,400	1,300	46,400	0	27,450	3,095	3,060	0	38,945	33,850	3,863	41,237	2,292	32,550	-1,293	46,393	7,448	0.13	0.08	-0.03
10	0	40,000	0	0	0	2,500	40,000	0	16,950	1,835	5,738	0	29,928	27,450	3,095	34,405	4,478	27,450	-1,905	39,405	9,478	0.19	0.08	-0.05
11	0	0	40,000	0	0	0	40,000	0	0	0	0	0	40,000	27,450	3,095	36,905	-3,095	27,450	-1,905	41,905	1,905	0.00	0.08	-0.05
12	0	0	0	40,000	0	2,500	40,000	0	27,450	3,095	0	0	34,405	27,450	3,095	34,405	0	27,450	95	37,405	3,000	0.08	0.08	0.00
13	80,000	0	0	0	6,400	1,300	86,400	0	67,450	10,588	6,120	0	68,393	72,550	12,837	72,263	3,871	72,550	13,965	71,136	2,743	0.19	0.15	0.16
14	0	80,000	0	0	0	7,700	80,000	0	43,750	5,374	11,062	0	55,865	59,750	9,381	62,919	7,054	59,750	9,869	62,432	6,567	0.21	0.12	0.12
15	0	0	40,000	40,000	0	0	80,000	0	61,450	9,268	0	0	70,733	67,450	11,460	68,540	-2,193	67,450	12,333	67,668	-3,065	0.12	0.14	0.15
16	0	0	0	80,000	0	7,700	80,000	0	59,750	8,894	0	0	63,407	59,750	9,381	62,919	-488	59,750	9,869	62,432	-975	0.11	0.12	0.12
17	160,000	0	0	0	6,400	1,300	166,400	18,000	142,000	28,101	11,174	0	125,825	152,550	38,388	126,712	887	152,550	46,143	118,957	-6,868	0.24	0.23	0.28
18	0	160,000	0	0	0	7,700	160,000	18,000	102,300	18,573	22,125	0	111,602	139,750	34,036	118,264	6,662	139,750	40,511	111,789	187	0.25	0.21	0.25
19	0	0	40,000	120,000	0	0	160,000	18,000	136,000	26,661	0	0	133,339	147,450	36,654	123,346	-9,993	147,450	43,899	116,101	-17,238	0.17	0.23	0.27
20	0	0	0	160,000	0	7,700	160,000	18,000	142,000	28,101	0	0	124,199	139,750	34,036	118,264	-5,935	139,750	40,469	111,832	-12,368	0.18	0.21	0.25

1/Employer premiums taxable under FTW and SSBI. For individuals with wages at or above $40K and Sched. C or unearned income >$40K, estimates from Kaiser 2021 Employer Health Benefits Survey, Figure B (All Plans). For Wages of $20K and Sched. C and Unearned incomes up to $40K, estimates use the Kaiser 2021 Health Insurance Marketplace Calculator. Those with incomes below $20K or OASDI income are assumed to be receiving Medicare or Medicaid. Individual Health Premiums not deductible for Wages, Sched. C and Unearned incomes at $20k and for Sched. C

2/Average from IRS Table 1.2 for highest group. Others take std.

3/Formulas differ for income types (columns B,C, D, & E)

4/Standard deduction only

Table 5.3 Net income and overall federal tax rates for married filers by income type and amount under SQ, FTW, and SSBI – including child allowance for two children

	Wages	Sched. C	OASDI	Unearned	Employer Health Premium 1/	Individual Health Premium 1/	Gross Income (incl. Emp. Health)	SQ Itemized 2/	SQ Taxable 1/3/	SQ FIT 4/	FICA 3/	SQ EITC	SQ Net	FTW Taxable 1/3/5/	FTW Tax	FTW Net	FTW Net - SQ Net	SSBI Taxable 1/3/	SSBI Tax	SSBI Net	SSBI Net - SQ Net	SQ Tax Rate	FTW Tax Rate	SSBI Tax Rate
1	20,000	0	0	0	0	0	20,000	0	0	-2,800	1,530	3,733	25,003	0	-10,000	30,000	4,997	0	-35,000	55,000	29,997	-0.25	-0.50	-1.75
2	0	20,000	0	0	0	0	20,000	0	0	-2,800	3,060	3,733	23,473	0	-10,000	30,000	6,527	0	-35,000	55,000	31,527	-0.17	-0.50	-1.75
3	0	0	20,000	0	0	0	20,000	0	0	-2,800	0	0	22,800	0	-10,000	30,000	7,200	0	-35,000	55,000	32,200	-0.14	-0.50	-1.75
4	0	0	0	20,000	0	0	20,000	0	0	-2,800	0	0	22,800	0	-10,000	30,000	7,200	0	-34,000	54,000	31,200	-0.14	-0.50	-1.70
5	40,000	0	0	0	0	0	40,000	0	14,900	-1,310	3,060	1,542	39,792	14,900	-7,510	47,510	7,718	14,900	-28,510	68,510	28,718	0.01	-0.19	-0.71
6	0	40,000	0	0	0	0	40,000	0	6,900	-2,110	6,120	1,542	37,532	14,900	-7,510	47,510	9,978	14,900	-28,510	68,510	30,978	0.06	-0.19	-0.71
7	0	0	40,000	0	0	0	40,000	0	0	-2,800	0	0	42,800	14,900	-7,510	47,510	4,710	14,900	-28,510	68,510	25,710	-0.07	-0.19	-0.71
8	0	0	0	40,000	0	0	40,000	0	14,900	-1,310	0	0	41,310	14,900	-7,510	47,510	6,200	14,900	-26,510	66,510	25,200	-0.03	-0.19	-0.66
9	80,000	0	0	0	16,200	0	96,200	0	54,900	2,190	6,120	0	81,890	71,100	4,754	85,446	3,556	65,100	-12,586	102,786	20,896	0.09	0.05	-0.13
10	0	80,000	0	0	0	4,900	80,000	0	38,900	270	11,490	0	63,340	54,900	1,190	73,910	10,570	54,900	-13,810	88,910	25,570	0.15	0.01	-0.17
11	0	0	80,000	0	0	0	80,000	0	14,900	-2,510	0	0	82,510	54,900	1,190	78,810	-3,700	54,900	-13,810	93,810	11,300	-0.03	0.01	-0.17
12	0	0	0	80,000	0	4,900	80,000	0	54,900	2,190	0	0	72,910	54,900	1,190	73,910	1,000	54,900	-9,810	84,910	12,000	0.03	0.01	-0.12
13	160,000	0	0	0	16,200	6,000	176,200	0	134,900	17,175	12,240	0	140,785	145,100	25,674	144,526	3,741	145,100	27,929	142,271	1,486	0.17	0.15	0.16
14	0	160,000	0	0	0	22,200	160,000	0	80,700	5,286	21,083	0	111,431	112,700	16,926	120,874	9,443	112,700	17,561	120,239	8,808	0.16	0.11	0.11
15	0	0	80,000	80,000	0	0	160,000	0	122,900	14,535	0	0	145,465	134,900	22,920	137,080	-8,385	134,900	24,665	135,335	-10,130	0.09	0.14	0.15
16	0		0	160,000	0	22,200	160,000	0	134,900	17,175	0	0	120,625	112,700	16,926	120,874	249	112,700	17,561	120,239	-386	0.11	0.11	0.11
17	320,000	0	0	0	16,200	6,000	336,200	31,000	289,000	53,402	22,978	0	253,820	305,100	76,776	253,424	-396	305,100	92,286	237,914	-15,906	0.23	0.23	0.27
18	0	320,000	0	0	0	22,200	320,000	31,000	202,800	32,714	40,910	0	224,176	272,700	65,760	232,040	7,864	272,700	78,030	219,770	-4,406	0.23	0.21	0.24
19	0	0	80,000	240,000	0	0	320,000	31,000	277,000	50,522	0	0	269,478	294,900	73,308	246,692	-22,786	294,900	87,798	232,202	-37,276	0.16	0.23	0.27
20	0	0	0	320,000	0	22,200	320,000	31,000	289,000	53,402	0	0	244,398	272,700	65,760	232,040	-12,358	272,700	78,030	219,770	-24,628	0.17	0.21	0.24

1/Employer premiums taxable under FTW and SSBI. For families with wages at or above $80K and Sched. C or unearned income >$80K, estimates from Kaiser 2021 Employer Health Benefits Survey, Figure B (All Plans) . For wages of $40K and Sched. C and Unearned incomes up to $80K, estimates use the Kaiser 2021 Health Insurance Marketplace Calculator. Those with incomes below $40K or OASDI income are assumed to be receiving Medicare or Medicaid. Individual Health Premiums not deductible for Wages, Sched. C and Unearned incomes at $40k and for Sched. C and Unearned incomes at $80K because premium estimates include tax credits.

2/Average from IRS Table 1.2 for highest group. Others take std.

3/Formulas differ for income types (columns B,C, D, & E)

4/Formulas differ for income levels due to limit of $1400 on refundable child tax credit.

5/Standard deduction only

113

Chapter 6. American Dream Reboot

For nearly a quarter of a millennium, we've relied on elected officials for the wisdom, leadership, resources, and technology needed to design and administer fair and effective rules that govern federal taxation and spending. They have failed us. The US budget is a runaway train that Congress has refused to slow down despite several decades of warnings by experts about the dire consequences of business as usual. Entitlements are blamed for budget deficits even as a trillion-dollar tax cut is passed to appease Wall Street. Enough is enough!

A system that served our grandparents will not serve our grandchildren, so it's high time we let it die of natural causes. We can do so much better than the payroll tax, which wasn't such a great idea to begin with but certainly doesn't work for today's economy. Boomers need to let go and trust younger generations to figure out what our country needs. It will not be difficult to improve upon Social Security, but it cannot be done without breaking the payroll tax chain that binds us to the past.

I may not live to see remedy of the root causes of the rot in our system, which lie in elections. But if voters get behind a big idea, politicians will follow. SSBI is a big idea. It solves a serious fiscal problem and makes a strong statement about American values. The Union was established to promote the general welfare (US Constitution 1787). Under current circumstances, nothing could be more relevant to our general welfare than a BIG. We have the resources and the capability to implement a fiscally responsible, flexible scheme that will provide financial security to all Americans. SSBI is carefully designed to be paid for by cuts to targeted deductions and moderate, progressive increases in federal income taxes. It is also designed to be adjusted with the Federal Poverty Guidelines. All of this is for naught if lawmakers can undermine the transfers by running large deficits. Therefore, we must insist that SSBI legislation include a balanced budget requirement that puts the income guarantee first and forces adjustments to discretionary budgets.

SSBI is very expensive; for that and many other reasons having to do mostly with threats to large taxpayers and tax spenders, it will be a lightning rod for controversy. People who have prospered under the SQ will fear loss of privileges and control. I expect ridicule and fearmongering from their camp. The thing is, we are doing a lot of other very expensive things for the benefit of special interests. Washington has become a feast for moneygrubbing rent-seekers, with no apparent limits to what Congress deems within its powers to spend or regulate. SSBI is no cure-all, but it is a very big step toward taking care of first things first. If we have enough money to send hundreds of thousands of soldiers to the Middle East, surely we have enough to feed a few million poor people living here in the US.

My analysis is crude insofar as it avoids entirely the macroeconomic effects of worker, employer, and investor behavioral responses.[60] Yet it is powerful because it addresses the main concern of every voter: What's in it for me? For the vast majority, the answer is *freedom*. The poor get a helping hand without work requirements and continue to get help if they find work. The middle class gets to decide when, how, and how much to save for their own retirement, and whatever they save is theirs (not an IOU from the SSA). Ten percenters (90th percentile income) will probably be surprised that they aren't hit harder by SSBI reforms. One percenters are hit pretty hard but should not be surprised. They will recover quickly because they are resourceful, enterprising people and because the millions of citizens getting SSBI payments will spend that money on goods and services – returning some tax dollars to those invested in the real economy.

Pay it Forward

The goal of making America great again clearly struck a nerve for millions in the 2016 Presidential election, and even those of us who do not share the nostalgia or cannot support policies that accompanied that vision can understand the sentiment. I've made many references to data that explain what was great about the middle of the last century compared to 2023. It's all about the middle class. Never mind all the gadgets and other "hedonic" improvements technology has delivered. Boomers remember when one salary supported a family and empty nesters could look forward to a secure retirement instead of worrying about debts, layoffs, a completely inadequate 401(k)

---

[60] Although I will defend the assumption of stasis by pointing to the estimated impact sections in Chapter 5. Neutrality of revenue and spending at the aggregate level and modest, positive effects on median taxpayer cash flows suggest that large transfers from rich to poor will not disrupt the economy as a whole. Budget discipline and more effective public spending will strengthen US competitiveness.

fund, and a Social Security system that looks like the game of musical chairs. Hardly anyone can say exactly what happened, but all of us can see that we lost something along the way.

The good old days many of us are pining for – the 1960s – featured the highest levels of trust in our institutions as well as the lowest levels of income inequality. Today, just 20 percent of Americans trust our federal government to do the right thing most of the time. Moreover, significant majorities believe Uncle Sam is doing too much for people with high incomes and too little for those with middle or low incomes (Pew 2022: 4, 53). Highly related to this trust deficit is extreme polarization of voters along the left-right divide created and fed by our two major parties. Each side is quick to blame the other. An extraordinary leader could help restore trust in our fellow Americans, but because our political system created the problem, it is unlikely to lead to election of such a person.[61]

Even if we started now, these political obstacles could take decades to clear, so how do we enact reforms needed to avert civil unrest and unnecessary suffering while we work on the trust issues? Popular opinion can shift quickly if we embrace a shared vision for a better future, but that is difficult to imagine happening when so many of us see the past and present differently. In recent years, numerous organizations have formed to address our political dysfunction; most of them provide civics education and encourage more dialogue and participation in government. So far, they don't seem to have made much difference. Civil discourse is desirable, but it will not necessarily change anyone's mind. Politics is about values, and we will never be able to agree on a path forward without a culture that respects differences in values. Recognizing, appreciating, and accommodating what others want will improve our capacity to imagine new roles and relationships. In this way, we can develop policies that, like trade in goods and services, allow everyone to participate in creating our future (McIntosh 2020)..

FTW/SSBI does just that; it's a hack that jump starts the process by focusing on potential mutual gains for all types of people that will make them less fearful and suspicious of radical change and, eventually, one another. Instead of trying to persuade people they should sacrifice for others, it shows how they will benefit themselves. When the vast majority are winners, we find change by consensus is worthy of celebration as the singular achievement of a healthy democracy. A 50-year-old white male who lost his manufacturing job may be, in terms of economic security,

---

[61] Gautam Mukunda (2012) put forth a theory that we have routinely filtered out leaders who would disrupt the status quo throughout our history and regardless of who was in power.

in the same boat as a 19-year-old single black mother. Likewise, a 35-year-old gay male immigrant coder and a 70-year-old widowed "church lady" may have the same comfortable incomes. Haters (and partisans) would have these people and their associates (friends, family, business colleagues, etc.) picking sides as to who deserves help on what terms, what form assistance should take, and who should pay for it. It's ugly enough to judge people based on characteristics; to judge their circumstances and decide that's all they will ever be is beyond cynical. It's a denial of the human spirit that makes all of us poorer.

The way forward is to look past stereotypes and differences rooted in age, sex, race, ethnicity, occupation, family status, religion, home, and lifestyle. We will all benefit from thinking less about why others are rich or poor and more about how our public institutions assist or hinder them. Some need a helping hand and others can afford to offer one. For many of us, especially under a more equitable tax code, that will change at some point in our lives. Fortune will smile on some and misfortune will visit others, and they may switch places along the way. Some people will make better choices and some will not, and they may switch places, too. The whole point of unconditional assistance and equally blind taxation methods like those I'm advocating is that we all deserve to find out for ourselves what we are capable of and what makes us happy.

Those on the receiving end will no longer have to beg, steal, or borrow just to survive. Basic needs will be affordable, additional income only reduces the basic income payment by one dollar for every four earned, and wages or self-employment earnings are no longer burdened by the payroll tax. And there is no stigma associated with the benefit because it is the same for every citizen 18 years or older. As optimistic as I am about SSBI, I am not so naïve as to think everyone who benefits will be grateful and behave accordingly. Too many people will remain addicted to substances and other habits such as blaming others for their circumstances and challenges. What will have changed is that every single one of us will have a chance. Those who seize the opportunity may influence others to do the same. Only the most isolated and truly hopeless individuals will fail to see that their fate is largely in their own hands.

SSBI does not guarantee availability of other forms of assistance, never mind a good job. While virtually all federal, state, and local public service providers will make adjustments, it is not at all obvious how they will do so. Significant variation in the design, funding, and operation of current programs will continue. All should see opportunity, though, in having so many citizens' basic needs paid for by the federal government. Some states and communities will find that they can offer more services to the most disadvantaged with the same resources, while others will make cuts to programs that are not critical. As they make these choices, residents will respond at the ballot box and in some cases by moving.

This is an important benefit of SSBI – giving not just individuals but communities more choices. To make it work, though, we must categorically deny the inevitable and overwhelming appeals to add cost of living adjustments, make exceptions to the age and citizenship requirements, and tack on amounts for special needs. If we believe in SSBI, we have to protect its integrity. The best way to undermine it would be to complicate it with a bunch of riders that make it an administrative and fiscal train wreck that doesn't really help the poor. SSBI can be a model of federalism – a national standard that relieves tremendous pressure on thousands of targeted social assistance programs – as long as it protects the freedom of all citizens. That will not happen if we reinforce and subsidize existing conditions, which is what we're really doing when we make exceptions. It doesn't matter if we make the SSBI amount $10,000 or $20,000 instead of $15,000 if that's what we are willing to pay for. What we cannot do is to make it $10,000 in Cleveland and $20,000 in San Francisco. We can also change the eligibility age (e.g., to 21). What we cannot do is make it 18 for some and 21 for others.

The solution to inequality cannot be a function of conditions that created inequality. This is the problem with the Fed's interest rate target and with systemic adjustments for inflation; they make it a self-fulfilling prophesy. Unless your objective is to keep property values, rents, and taxes high, it makes no sense to adjust welfare payments by location. People won't move to cheaper areas if doing so reduces their income. Fixed federal assistance to residents in high cost areas gives them the option of using the money to stay put (near their workplace) or to find a cheaper place – maybe even in another state – and pocket the savings.[62] Landlords may capture some of the SSBI payments through higher rents; the important thing is that renters aren't stuck with location-based benefits. State and local governments can make up the difference if they get enough pressure to maintain the status quo. Cost of living adjustments that provide higher federal payments to those in urban communities add to inequality and undermine efforts to reduce it.

Those on the giving end of SSBI will know that they are getting the same nominal benefit as everyone else, with the only difference being who gets a check based on

---

[62] Jenny Schuetz (2018) lists do's and don'ts of housing policy that include providing income support to poor families and avoiding subsidies and other supply-side policies that are inefficient and distort markets. An Urban Institute study found that cash assistance offers renters more access, flexibility, efficiency, and choice as a supplement to housing support programs (Bogle et al. 2022).

current income. No one will be quite as dependent on unemployment insurance or savings to get through a job or career transition, whether or not it's voluntary. Of course, not everyone will see it that way. Some will resent paying taxes on Social Security and FI surtaxes that wind up in the pockets of people who aren't working, didn't go to college, and may not live or vote the way they "should." The resentful taxpayers may have lost deductions for large, illiquid investments such as homes and businesses – commitments that were made under a reasonable assumption that tax laws would remain favorable. As someone who is not really a fan of government in general and taxation in particular, I get it. And no one likes losing something they feel they have earned "fair and square." However, at the risk of sounding flippant, my answer is that it's time to grow up.

First of all, we can afford it. No one paying additional taxes (SSBI vs. SQ) is going to go broke due to SSBI alone. One-percenters living on the edge (i.e., drowning in debt with no liquid assets) have only themselves to blame. Secondly, people who inherit or earn megabucks should know better. If we are to have any hope of self-government, those who are capable of taking care of themselves must do so. That would seem to apply automatically to people with high six figure incomes that presumably reflect or command the trust of employers, employees, customers, investors, and their families. Sophisticated players know how to hedge their bets and protect their resources, and they know better than anyone how fragile policy can be. Some of them have not just taken advantage of policies as written; they have helped enact, revise, repeal, or defend those policies. SSBI is overdue, and some who could be categorized as losers in the transition should consider themselves fortunate the party lasted as long as it has. Just as many net beneficiaries will not make the best of their new opportunities, many net contributors will not fare well despite their vast advantages. That is on them.

Erasing the Work/Welfare Divide

If the work ethic is wanting, it's because we have robbed work of its dignity through policies that throw money at those with means while forcing everyone else to supply whatever labor has not yet been outsourced. The answer is not to cease trade or raise the minimum wage; both would treat symptoms and ultimately harm workers. We must reverse course with an organic approach that eliminates poverty. Inequality is a fact of life, but it should not be an outcome of public policy. We have reinforced conditions of inequality by favoring citizens with access to credit and imposing conditions on those who need a helping hand. Let's remove the debt subsidies and place public assistance at the top of federal spending priorities with SSBI.

The implication of our work ethic extends far beyond labor and responsibility as habits or obligations. By equating identity with work, work with a job, and jobs with 40 hours, health care and pension benefits, and a career, we created a measure of success that may do more damage than good. It divides the haves from the have-nots, which is particularly harmful in an era when changes in the nature of work relationships makes all these features of traditional jobs increasingly obsolete. The poor are already hurting, but sooner or later the failure to adjust our expectations about work will become a serious problem for our society as a whole. Even as the whole world of work changes before our eyes, we've doubled down on the 20th century paradigm. Millions of young entrepreneurs, professionals, and executives have prospered and millions of others who had no other choice have adapted and even prospered in this period of rapid change despite public policy failures. But as we grow older and experience slower economic growth, it will become painfully obvious that we need new tools.

I'm referring to more than just the BIG safety net. SSBI is funded in large part by removing most tax expenditures not just to raise revenue but to shift the inequality equation. For example, deductibility of employer paid health insurance favors employers who still provide traditional jobs with medical and retirement benefits. Those jobs are disappearing, and they might be even less prevalent if employees were not tethered to them by health benefits. Is this good policy – to help employers hold their employees hostage? Why not put the benefit in the hands of the employee? This is the intent of the FTW provisions to make employer paid medical insurance premiums taxable and individual insurance and health care expenses deductible. Under FTW or SSBI, workers would still benefit from employer paid insurance. Paying taxes on premiums is much cheaper than paying the premiums. However, by increasing transparency and raising stakes for employees, it would increase competition between employers, health insurance companies, and providers. Health insurance premiums have risen faster than workers' earnings since the turn of the century (Claxton 2018: 41) and total expenditures on health care as a percentage of GDP is projected to continue growing rapidly over the next decade (Statista 2022). Something must give. The industry and Congress gave it their best shot with ACA and managed to increase coverage but failed to get spending under control. It's time to put it in consumers' hands. With more skin in the game and exit options, taxpayers may have enough market power to persuade the health care industry to offer plans that follow individuals through changes in location, occupation, industry, etc.[63]

How about education? Are we really helping the average American by encouraging college attendance when so many students emerge buried in debt and without a degree, with a degree and no job, or with a job that does not pay enough to service their student loan or replace lost earnings? FTW and SSBI discontinue tax deductions for education because it is not a safety net component.[64] Education policy is just as prominent an indicator of our misguided work ethic as work requirements for welfare. Education has enjoyed sacred cow status for generations, but it is eating our lunch as a jobs strategy because, as with health care, we are spending more than ever and far more than other countries despite evidence that marginal returns are terrible (Caplan 2018, Markovits 2019: 153-6). Statistically, higher education correlates with employment and earnings, so we infer that everyone should get a degree. But jobs are not a function of worker demand; they match employer demand with workers on the supply side. Even (maybe especially) non-economists can see where this is going. Uncle Sam encourages everyone to pursue secondary education even when fiscal and monetary policies are encouraging capital investments that reduce demand for American workers. In the short run, as workers seek more education, their labor is taken off the market and the unemployment rate is lower. In the long run, though, the number of jobs is unchanged; employers hire more people with degrees to do the same work those without degrees were doing before.

Large employers with specific needs used to train their own employees; today they tell colleges what to teach if they want students to get jobs when they graduate. It works quite well for everyone but the students, many of whom enroll but don't get the jobs, and taxpayers whose dollars (inefficiently) subsidized education providers and employers while giving false hope to many students. That's actually a charitable view of it. When people have little chance of getting any job without advanced education or training, they can feel forced into additional study courses or training programs. This system is a creature of the work ethic because it equates financial security with jobs and jobs with education. Take away the federally funded (forced) labor supply, and employers will have to provide scholarships, promise jobs, and pay decent salaries to get people to forgo other opportunities and put in the extra time.

---

[63] States regulate insurance, so geographic portability can be complicated. However, this is yet another example of federalism at work. This single change in federal policy can help create new standards that protect individual rights and choice with many variations between plans and employer roles.

[64] Tax expenditures on education were approximately $30 billion in 2021 (US Treasury 2023).

Middle Class Solidarity

Opposition to welfare can get ugly because some believe they are working to pay for others' indolence. Conservatives have fanned these flames of indignation by suggesting that it's game over if the majority can vote for more benefits paid for by the minority. Any proposal to expand welfare in the US, and especially one as ambitious as mine, must overcome this obstacle. The "hack" I suggested at the beginning of this chapter is to break it down into ideological and practical components and start with the practical. The ideological (and tribal) reaction to taking something from "us" to give to "them" can only be overcome by a cosmopolitan, developmental perspective in which we respect differences and accept at face value policies that benefit all of us in the same way. SSBI uses universal benefits to blur the lines between givers and takers that keep us divided.

I know better than to expect many of the 1 percent or even the 10 percent to embrace SSBI in principle or in practice, because many of them will lose cherished tax breaks and pay higher taxes. Yet I'm idealistic enough to think the 90 percent can and will – over a generation or two, mind you – accept the challenge of self-government and stop exploitation of workers by the ruling class. SSBI will be difficult for many to grasp and accept because it is just about the opposite of the system we have experienced, one that virtually all of our leaders have defended and even "strengthened" because it has become its own American institution. Social Security was carefully designed and sold as anything but welfare, but SSBI is clearly and unapologetically so. Most of us are entitled to Social Security benefits; many will find it difficult to accept that we are more dependent on it than anyone will be on SSBI.

As explained in Chapter 5, the payroll tax creates the entitlement, and its tangled web snares about 200 million contributors and beneficiaries every year. By contrast, under SSBI, dependency is a function of individuals' circumstances; roughly half as many would receive payments. Moreover, those payments are determined one year at a time. Millions of workers will move in and out, up and down the continuum of people who are paying taxes or receiving SSBI payments in the range of annual incomes up to about $100,000. Sure, some will be stuck in one place, for one reason or another and for better or worse. But the new system opens up so many more possibilities for all of us because we are all promised the same thing as everyone else, every year. It will go a long way toward lifting the stigma of public assistance if individuals and families earning several times the Federal Poverty Guidelines are receiving benefits and no one has to endure the indignity of an application process. It will also help silence the righteous claims of older beneficiaries that their welfare payments were earned. Ironically, we will be freer if everyone is eligible for welfare, and we will be a lot less likely to judge one another on the basis of income or work status.

Second, while I think it is a marvel of simplicity compared to our current tax code and array of social welfare programs, chances are that many will balk at the negative income tax structure and the surtaxes that make it work – again, mainly because it is just so different from what we're accustomed to and also because special interests will attack the scheme by any means necessary. I needed to crunch the numbers to test feasibility and fine tune formulas, but the main reason I prepared the tables and charts in Chapter 5 is to be as transparent as possible with the data. Design of SSBI is intended to be neutral at the macro level and to minimize disruption of plans by individuals and households. It goes without saying that change will be opposed by those who stand to lose by paying higher taxes. That's a feature, not a bug, for the 10 percent, but SSBI is intended to minimize transfers between the 90 percenters. Major adjustments are accounted for with reasonable assumptions to show that for average middle-income taxpayers, i.e., those without extraordinary deductions, SSBI will have no significant negative impact on net incomes. Examples in Chapter 5 show those concerned about retirement planning that payroll tax savings can be used to further reduce income taxes and secure an asset instead of an IOU in the form of a benefit projection from SSA. These arguments should overcome most objections coming from the middle class. Even if they don't like the idea of a BIG, why would they oppose it if they stand to benefit, as well?

We have so far to go in taking our country back. SSBI is, honestly, just the beginning. It's a catch-all program that would be much smaller if our elected officials had not sold us out so long ago. Poverty persists and the middle class is under siege; full implementation of SSBI will take decades, and it will take much longer to recover and repair the damage. Ask anyone who was raised in a poor household, has declared bankruptcy, or has been unemployed for over a year or for many shorter periods. Savings that took years to accumulate are depleted in months and debts accumulated in months take years to erase. Worn-out goods take years to replace. Schooling, moving, raising a family, starting a business, and other aspirational goals take even longer to achieve if we are fortunate enough to turn the corner on financial security. SSBI will help many of us recover from mismanagement of the US economy and it will prevent catastrophic damage from future mistakes. But ideally, we will not stop there.

Having declared "enough" as a result of recognizing the destruction wrought by regressive monetary and tax policies, We the People need to follow through by reversing as many of them as possible. They are too numerous to mention and some will die a natural death as the benefits are taxed away under SSBI. Job 1 for voters, though, is to insist that their Members of Congress balance budgets with discretionary funding. Tax revenues must cover SSBI and other mandatory spending (e.g., Medicare) before the customary logrolling begins on other budget items. Because deficit spending leads to borrowing and money printing that destroys the value of each dollar, it will poke holes in the new safety net. Any changes to the SSBI should be made only after transparent and fully informed public hearings to review the tax rate schedule and fully funded discretionary spending options. In other words, we should all say, "Go ahead and fund your pet programs as long as our basic needs are taken care of." We are not used to making choices; we've become far too complacent with $1 trillion deficits because we've survived many in the hundred-billion range and none of us want to pay more or get less. I hope you are convinced that debt is not our friend. It benefits the ruling class at the expense of the working class. If we have to choose funding our BIG or program X, the BIG will win every time. With no budget discipline, SSBI will be disappointing.

Having finally seen to it that our federal taxes provide for basic needs of all adult citizens, we should reconsider other priorities. There should be far less need to fight multiple budget battles for aid components like housing, food, and health care that the BIG has rendered more affordable. In any event, these should become state and local concerns. Unemployment Compensation is a good example of a program that will likely continue but become much smaller and more affordable in the BIG context. Many other federally funded benefit programs will see reduced demand. States may continue to supplement the BIG, perhaps by providing services instead of income support, depending on local needs. Advocates of such programs may no longer need to support programs they don't care about to obtain others' votes (logrolling). With SSBI, voters can say "No" to the "job creators" who forced them to work and to Congressmen who demanded votes for their continued support of poverty relief programs.

I'm agnostic on non-cash public assistance; I can only surmise that the effect of providing many more needy people a lot of money will reduce the number of needy people and needs in general. That may lead to focusing more services on the neediest populations or it may lead to cuts in services and taxes. Those are decisions for others to make. They will be difficult, and for many the first response will be to ask the entity that can print money to save them from having to make those choices. The most vocal parties will likely be special interests that have lost out because they relied upon federal programs or tax deductions that are gone under FTW or SSBI reforms.

They will be joined by individuals who want to have their cake and eat it, too – people who will enjoy net increases in benefits but want to keep the old ones. Some of those getting the most assistance will be unemployed or underemployed and they may spend their spare time to pester elected officials who are already inclined toward federal government solutions to state and local problems. This lesson is larger than the payroll tax; there are many other federal interventions that have worsened income inequality. If we fail to recognize that and leave untouched or restore the many exceptions that could undermine reform, it will fail.

Federal programs that demonstrate effectiveness in the SSBI environment will survive. Those too small to matter will probably survive, also. Those wasting tens of billions of dollars that could increase the BIG or reduce the FI surtax should not. The flexibility of SSBI combined with the discipline of a balanced budget changes the budget game from blaming entitlements to owning them and taking responsibility for protecting not just payment of benefits but integrity of the dollar and the tax system that maintains its value.

Ten Years After

> I'd love to change the world
> But I don't know what to do
> So I'll leave it up to you
> > – Alvin Lee (1971)

This is the refrain of an incredible song from another troubled period in US history. Things changed but not the way many were hoping they would. After writing thousands of words in support of a very specific solution to an enormous (and persistent) problem, it seems appropriate to take a step back and admit that I am not sure of anything. This book is an expression of my concerns and my ideas. I hope others are inspired to question, criticize, investigate, and offer counter-proposals. But whether and how the world changes aren't up to me or to those who read this book; change of this magnitude will require self-government – deliberate action by the American people to protect our rights.

Today is Martin Luther King Day. A friend shared on Facebook a quote from one of the reverend's speeches that provided yet another reminder of how long ago this enormous problem was identified and how little progress we have made. I read the speech and saw this: "Socialism for the rich and Capitalism for the poor." Sound familiar? Here's more: "It is this moral lag in our thing-oriented society that blinds us to the human reality around us and encourages us in the greed and exploitation which creates the sector of poverty in the midst of wealth. Again, we have deluded ourselves into believing the myth that Capitalism grew and prospered out of the protestant ethic of hard work and sacrifice; the fact is that Capitalism was built on the exploitation and suffering of black slaves and continues to thrive on the exploitation of the poor – both black and white, both here and abroad." And finally,

So, we are here because we believe, we hope, we pray that something new might emerge in the political life of this nation which will produce a new man, new structures and new institutions and a new life for mankind. I am convinced that this new life will not emerge until our nation undergoes a radical revolution of values. When machines and computers, profit motives and property rights are considered more important than people the giant triplets of racism, economic exploitation and militarism are incapable of being conquered. A civilization can flounder as readily in the face of moral bankruptcy as it can through financial bankruptcy. A true revolution of values will soon cause us to question the fairness and justice of many of our past and present policies…. A true revolution of values will soon look uneasily on the glaring contrast of poverty and wealth, with righteous indignation it will look at thousands of working people displaced from their jobs, with reduced incomes as a result of automation while the profits of the employers remain intact and say, this is not just…. A nation that continues year after year, to spend more money on military defense than on programs of social uplift is approaching spiritual death (King 1967).

When Dr. King made this speech, I was ten years old and starting 5th grade at Dufrocq Elementary School in Baton Rouge, LA. Two years earlier, my family had lost our home in Larose to Hurricane Betsy and moved to the city to stay with my grandmother in her small house on Convention St., a brick street lined with pecan trees very close to downtown. When our parents found work, we moved into a nearby apartment and my younger sister and I continued to walk a little over a mile each day to and from school. We did not know why, but in three years, our school population went from about 90 percent white to 90 percent black. One day in the fall of 1968, my sister and I both got in completely unrelated fights with black kids. We were suspended and my father was so upset about it, he would not let us return and we moved to the suburbs, which is apparently where all the other white families had gone. A year after that, my parents divorced and I moved to Houston with my father. I had played football in Baton Rouge and looked forward to playing for Johnston Jr. High. The day after getting my uniform and three days before school began, I was told that because of desegregation, I would have to attend Fondren Jr. High, instead, which was two miles further from our apartment. It made no sense to me, especially since there wasn't any diversity to speak of in either school. I quit football. The next year I moved again and took up soccer, but the point is that as children, my sister and I were already dealing with plenty of family drama; the politics of race in the South just added to it. My guess is that our story is not that unusual for families of modest means, black or white. What we learned was that mixing races caused trouble.

Fast forward about 50 years and anecdotally, not much has changed in the South. Fortunately, I've changed. In college and especially in my two decades in the Washington, DC area, I've met, worked with, and studied many races and cultures, and I find the diversity as interesting and rewarding as it is challenging at times. But not everyone has the opportunities I have had, nor will everyone take the same path. It will take much more than mixing races to eliminate racism. Dr. King's insight was that we needed "a radical revolution of values." We still do. What does that mean? He told us to "look uneasily on the glaring contrast of poverty and wealth." I am uneasy about it because it indicates unnecessary suffering – not just the possibility of relief but the possibility that it could have been prevented.

Redistribution of income treats the symptoms, but it does not necessarily treat the disease of prejudice. It is highly likely to further divide us, because so many of us believe welfare is shameful and taxation is theft. What's so wrong with this is that wealth affords preferential treatment. "Possession is 9/10 of the law" is a saying that aptly describes our perverse tax policy of requiring employers to withhold the first 15 cents of every worker's earnings while employers and their shareholders pay taxes on the honor system. The message, which is reinforced by virtually all welfare policies in our country, is that poor people cannot be trusted. Some people may believe it's because they deserve to be poor as punishment for past deeds or because they are unwilling to earn their keep. Some may believe it's because they are desperate and likely to lie or take advantage of others to escape their predicament. Poor people in the US are not all black or Hispanic but those who are black or Hispanic are more likely to be poor. This means prejudice against the poor hides racist motives. Not all of those who do not trust the poor are racist, but I would wager most racists do not trust the poor.

For half a century, public policies have treated poverty and race separately.[65] It appears to me that one reason we have made so little progress on either is that we tried to have it both ways – pretending to help everyone (with antidiscrimination laws) while holding back on welfare and other forms of assistance that might allow poor

---

[65] Ibram Kendi (2019: 156-63), also citing Dr. King, says racism and capitalism are "conjoined twins" that will live or die together. It is naïve, he says, to fight them independently.

blacks and immigrants to climb into the middle class. It seems counterintuitive, but I believe the way out is to focus on a colorblind policy to alleviate poverty. SSBI is a direct challenge to the ideas that poor people do not deserve help and cannot be trusted. It isn't even an appeal to sympathy for the poor. The premise of the BIG is that *all of us* are deserving and trustworthy. Federal, state, and local governments have myriad tools to deal with exceptions – those who need more and those who abuse our trust. My hope is that by weaving into the fabric of our most fundamental interaction with all other American citizens a meaningful commitment to equality, all of us may find greater justice and peace.

Bibliography

Alpert, Daniel, et al. (2019) "The U.S. Private Sector Job Quality Index," Cornell Law School White Paper (https://ubwp.buffalo.edu/job-quality-index-jqi/wp-content/uploads/sites/171/2021/08/jqi-white-paper.pdf)

Alston, Philip (2018) "Report of the Special Rapporteur on extreme poverty and human rights on his mission to the United States of America," United Nations Human Rights Council, Thirty-eighth session, Agenda item 3 (http://undocs.org/A/HRC/38/33/ADD.1)

Anderson, Elizabeth (2016) "Common Property: How Social Insurance Became Confused with Socialism," *Boston Review*, July 25, 2016 (http://bostonreview.net/us-books-ideas/elizabeth-anderson-common-property)

Atkinson, Anthony B. (2015) *Inequality: What Can Be Done?*, Cambridge: Harvard University Press

Autor, David, David A. Mindell, and Elisabeth B. Reynolds (2019) *The Work of the Future: Shaping Technology and Institutions*, MIT Task Force on the Work of the Future (https://workofthefuture.mit.edu/wp-content/uploads/2020/08/WorkoftheFuture_Report_Shaping_Technology_and_Institutions.pdf?cb=4e516bdd)

Bacevich, Andrew J. (2016) *America's War for the Greater Middle East*, New York: Random House

______ (2020) *The Age of Illusions: How America Squandered its Cold War Victory*, New York: Metropolitan Books

Bach, Wendy A. (2017) "Poor Support/Rich Support: (Re)Viewing the American Social Welfare State," University of Tennessee Legal Studies Research Paper No. 317, *Florida Tax Review*, 2017 (https://papers.ssrn.com/sol3/papers.cfm?abstract_id=2970198)

Badger, Emily (2017) "Why Work Requirement Became a Theme of the Trump Budget," *The New York Times,* May 24, 2017 (https://www.nytimes.com/2017/05/24/upshot/why-work-requirement-became-a-theme-of-the-trump-budget.html?ref=economy&_r=1)

Barnes, Mitchell, et al. (2021) *The Social Insurance System in the U.S.: Policies to Protect Workers and Families*, The Hamilton Project (https://www.brookings.edu/wp-content/uploads/2021/06/Social-Insurance-FP_v4.5.pdf)

Bar-Yam, Yaneer, et al (2018) "Preliminary steps toward a universal economic dynamics for monetary and fiscal policy," New England Complex Systems Institute (https://arxiv.org/pdf/1710.06285.pdf)

Beckett, Andy (2018) "Post-work: the radical idea of a world without jobs," *The Guardian*, January 19, 2018 (https://www.theguardian.com/news/2018/jan/19/post-work-the-radical-idea-of-a-world-without-jobs)

Bergstein, Brian (2018) "Basic Income Could Work—if You Do it Canada-Style," *MIT Technology Review*, June 21, 2018 (https://medium.com/mit-technology-review/basic-income-could-work-if-you-do-it-canada-style-2d483e733165)

Bidadanure, Juliana Uhuru (2019) "The Political Theory of Universal Basic Income," *Annual Review of Political Science* 22:481-501 (https://www.annualreviews.org/doi/10.1146/annurev-polisci-050317-070954)

Biggs, Andrew, et al. (2016) *Increasing the Effectiveness and Sustainability of the Nation's Entitlement Programs*, American Enterprise Institute for Public Policy Research (http://www.aei.org/wp-content/uploads/2016/06/Increasing-the-Effectiveness.pdf)

Bivens, Josh, and Hunter Blair (2017) *"Competitive" distractions*, Economic Policy Institute (https://www.epi.org/files/pdf/114189.pdf)

Block, Fred, and Frances Fox Piven (2016) "A Basic Income Would Upend America's Work Ethic—and That's a Good Thing," *The Nation*, August 23, 2016 (https://www.thenation.com/article/archive/a-basic-income-would-upend-americas-work-ethic-and-thats-a-good-thing/)

Boccia, Romina (2017) *A Social Security Primer for the New Administration: Reform Needed Now*, Heritage Foundation Report (https://www.heritage.org/social-security/report/social-security-primer-the-new-administration-reform-needed-now)

Bogle, Mary, et al. (2022) *Guaranteed Income as a Mechanism for Promoting Housing Stability*, Urban Institute Research Report (https://www.urban.org/research/publication/guaranteed-income-mechanism-promoting-housing-stability)

Booth, Danielle DiMartino (2017) *Fed Up: An Insider's Take on Why the Federal Reserve Is Bad for America*, New York: Portfolio Penguin

Boushey, Heather (2019a) *Unbound: How Inequality Constricts Our Economy and What We Can Do About It*, Cambridge: Harvard University Press

_______ (2019b) Testimony before the House Budget Committee, Hearing on "Solutions to Rising Economic Inequality," September 19, 2019

(https://equitablegrowth.org/testimony-by-heather-boushey-before-the-house-budget-committee/)

Brazeal, Gregory (2023) "Markets as Legal Constructions," *University of Cincinnati Law Review* 91:3 (https://scholarship.law.uc.edu/uclr/vol91/iss3/1/)

Brenan, Megan (2023) "Americans' Outlook for Their Retirement Has Worsened," The Gallup Organization (https://news.gallup.com/poll/506330/americans-outlook-retirement-worsened.aspx)

Breunig, Elizabeth (2018) "If the poor must work to earn every dollar, shouldn't the rich?," The Washington Post, January 5, 2018 (https://www.washingtonpost.com/opinions/if-the-poor-must-work-to-earn-every-dollar-shouldnt-the-rich/2018/01/05/c36d9a10-f243-11e7-b390-a36dc3fa2842_story.html?noredirect=on&utm_term=.3dad7659d4b0)

Bricker, Jesse, et al. (2017) "Changes in U.S. Family Finances from 2013 to 2016: Evidence from the Survey of Consumer Finances," *Federal Reserve Bulletin* 103:3 (https://www.federalreserve.gov/publications/files/scf17.pdf)

Burman, Leonard E., Eric Toder, and Christopher Geissler (2008) "How Big Are Total Individual Income Tax Expenditures, and Who Benefits from Them?," American Social Science Associations Discussion Paper No. 31 (https://www.taxpolicycenter.org/sites/default/files/alfresco/publication-pdfs/1001234-How-Big-Are-Total-Individual-Income-Tax-Expenditures-and-Who-Benefits-from-Them-.PDF)

Burtless, Gary, and Sveta Milusheva (2013) "Effects of Employer-Sponsored Health Insurance Costs on Social Security Taxable Wages," *Social Security Bulletin* 73:1 (https://www.ssa.gov/policy/docs/ssb/v73n1/v73n1p83.pdf)

Butcher, Kristin F., and Diane Whitmore Schanzenbach (2018) "Most Workers in Low-Wage Labor Market Work Substantial Hours, in Volatile Jobs: SNAP or Medicaid Work Requirements Would Be Difficult for Many Low-Wage Workers to Meet," Center on Budget and Policy Priorities (https://www.cbpp.org/sites/default/files/atoms/files/7-24-18pov.pdf)

Caplan, Bryan (2018) *The Case against Education: Why the Education System Is a Waste of Time and Money*, Princeton: Princeton University Press

Capretta, James C. (2015) "Why Not Cut the Payroll Tax?," *National Review*, February 13, 2015 (https://www.nationalreview.com/2015/02/why-not-cut-payroll-tax-james-c-capretta/)

Cass, Oren (2013) "The Height of the Net," *National Review*, October 14, 2013 (https://www.nationalreview.com/magazine/2013/10/14/height-net/)

______ (2018) *The Once and Future Worker: A Vision for the Renewal of Work in America*, New York: Encounter Books.

Chalabi, Mona (2016) "The 'war on drugs' in numbers: a systematic failure of policy," *The Guardian*, April 19, 2016 (https://www.theguardian.com/world/2016/apr/19/war-on-drugs-statistics-systematic-policy-failure-united-nations)

Chien, Nina, et al. (2021) *Risks that Come with Increasing Earnings for Low-Income Workers Receiving Safety Net Programs: Perspectives of Working Parents*, Department of Health and Human Services, Office of the Assistance Secretary of Planning and Evaluation (https://aspe.hhs.gov/sites/default/files/documents/04efcaa192583caf5f53b98b80802ca6/MTR_Qual_Study_Brief_Risks.pdf)

Clancy, Dean (2015) "The Best Way to Reform Social Security," *U.S. News &World Report*, April 27, 2015 (https://www.usnews.com/opinion/blogs/opinion-blog/2015/04/27/the-best-way-to-reform-social-security-eliminate-the-payroll-tax)

Claxton, Gary, et al. (2022) *Employer Health Benefits 2022 Annual Survey*, The Kaiser Family Foundation and Health Insurance & Educational Trust (https://files.kff.org/attachment/Report-Employer-Health-Benefits-2022-Annual-Survey.pdf)

Committee for a Responsible Federal Budget (2023) "Analysis of the 2023 Medicare Trustees' Report," April 3, 2023 (https://www.crfb.org/papers/analysis-2023-medicare-trustees-report)

Concord Coalition (2005) "The Future of Social Security," Testimony for the U.S. Senate Special Committee on Aging, February 3, 2005 (https://www.aging.senate.gov/imo/media/doc/hr136rb.pdf)

Coontz, Stephanie (2014) "The New Instability," *The New York Times*, July 26, 2014 (https://www.nytimes.com/2014/07/27/opinion/sunday/the-new-instability.html?_r)

DeSilver, Drew (2023) "Who pays, and doesn't pay, federal income taxes in the U.S.?," Pew Research Center, April, 18, 2023 (https://www.pewresearch.org/short-reads/2023/04/18/who-pays-and-doesnt-pay-federal-income-taxes-in-the-us/)

Desmond, Matthew (2023) *Poverty, By America*, New York: Crown

Dewey, Caitlin, and Tracy Jan (2017) "Trump to poor Americans: Get to work or lose your benefits," *The Washington Post*, May 22, 2017 (https://www.washingtonpost.com/news/wonk/wp/2017/05/22/trump-to-

poor-americans-get-to-work-or-lose-your-
benefits/?noredirect=on&utm_term=.f417101d30d9)

Diamond, Peter, and Emmanuel Saez (2011) "The Case for a Progressive Tax: From Basic Research to Policy Recommendations," *Journal of Economic Perspectives* 25:4 (https://pubs.aeaweb.org/doi/pdfplus/10.1257/jep.25.4.165)

Dolan, Ed (2018) "Earning It: Why work requirements don't work," Milken Institute Review (http://www.milkenreview.org/articles/earning-it-why-work-requirements-dont-work)

Dorfman, Jeffrey (2015) "Don't Tax The Rich To Benefit The Middle Class, Help The Poor Instead," *Forbes*, January 22, 2015 (https://www.forbes.com/sites/jeffreydorfman/2015/01/22/dont-tax-the-rich-to-benefit-the-middle-class-help-the-poor-instead/?sh=400929b24877)

Dougherty, Conor (2018) "Why Rent Control Is a Lightning Rod," *The New York Times*, October 12, 2018 (https://www.nytimes.com/2018/10/12/business/economy/rent-control-explained.html)

Duflo, Esther, and Abhijit Banerjee (2019) "Economic Incentives Don't Always Do What We Want Them To," *The New York Times*, October 26, 2019 (https://www.nytimes.com/2019/10/26/opinion/sunday/duflo-banerjee-economic-incentives.html?action=click&module=RelatedLinks&pgtype=Article&utm_campaign=Economic%20Studies&utm_source=hs_email&utm_medium=email&utm_content=79356518)

Durkheim, Emile (1984) *The Division of Labor in Society*, trans. W.D. Halls, New York: The Free Press

Evans, David K., and Anna Popova (2014) "Cash Transfers and Temptation Goods: A Review of Global Evidence," The World Bank, Policy Research Working Paper 6886 (http://documents.worldbank.org/curated/en/617631468001808739/pdf/WPS6886.pdf)

Federal Reserve Board (2021a) Survey of Consumer Finances, 1989-2019, Before-tax family income by age of reference person (https://www.federalreserve.gov/econres/scf/dataviz/scf/chart/#series:Before_Tax_Income;demographic:agecl;population:all;units:median)

_______ (2021b) Survey of Consumer Finances, 1989-2019, Retirement accounts by age of reference person (https://www.federalreserve.gov/econres/scf/dataviz/scf/chart/#series:Retire

ment_Accounts;demographic:agecl;population:1,2,3,4,5,6;units:median;range:198
9,2019)

Fortson, Kenneth, et al. (2017) *Providing Public Workforce Services to Job Seekers: 30-Month Impact Findings on the WIA Adult and Dislocated Worker Programs,* Washington, DC: Mathematica Policy Research (https://www.mathematica-mpr.com/our-publications-and-findings/publications/providing-public-workforce-services-to-job-seekers-30-month-impact-findings-on-the-wia-adult)

Frey, Carl Benedikt (2019) *The Technology Trap: Capital, Labor, and Power in the Age of Automation,* Princeton: Princeton University Press

Friedman, Milton (1962) *Capitalism and Freedom,* Chicago, IL: University of Chicago Press

Gabler, Neal (2016) "The Secret Shame of Middle-Class Americans," The Atlantic, May 2016 (https://www.theatlantic.com/magazine/archive/2016/05/my-secret-shame/476415/)

Gale, William G., and Claire Haldeman (2021) *The Tax Cuts and Jobs Act: Searching for supply-side effects,* (https://www.brookings.edu/wp-content/uploads/2021/07/20210628_TPC_GaleHaldeman_TCJASupplySideEffectsReport_FINAL.pdf)

Gallup (2023) Party Affiliation (https://news.gallup.com/poll/15370/party-affiliation.aspx)

Garfinkel, I., Chien-Chung Huang, and Wendy Naidich (2006) "The effects of a basic income guarantee on poverty and income distribution" In Bruce Ackerman, Anne Alstott, & Philipe Van Parijs (edited by Erik Olin Wright), *Redesigning Distribution: Basic Income and Stakeholder Grants as Cornerstones for an Egalitarian Capitalism,* London: Verso

Gould, Elise (2015) "2014 Continues a 35-Year Trend of Broad-Based Wage Stagnation," Issue Brief #393, Economic Policy Institute (https://www.epi.org/publication/stagnant-wages-in-2014/)

Graeber, David (2014) *Debt: The First 5,000 Years,* Brooklyn: Melville House
______ (2018) *Bullshit Jobs,* New York: Simon & Schuster

Graeber, David, and David Wengrow (2021) *The Dawn of Everything: A New History of Humanity,* New York: Farrar, Strauss, and Giroux

Greenstein, Bob (2017) "Commentary: Universal Basic Income May Sound Attractive But, If It Occurred, Would Likelier Increase Poverty Than Reduce It," Center on Budget and Policy Priorities (https://www.cbpp.org/sites/default/files/atoms/files/5-31-16bud.pdf)

Griffin, Riley (2018) "The Student Loan Debt Crisis Is About to Get Worse," Bloomberg Personal Finance, October 17, 2018 (https://www.bloomberg.com/news/articles/2018-10-17/the-student-loan-debt-crisis-is-about-to-get-worse)

Gruber, Jonathan (2010) "The Tax Exclusion for Employer-Sponsored Health Insurance," National Bureau of Economic Research, Working Paper 15766 (http://www.nber.org/papers/w15766.pdf)

Gwynne, Kristen (2018) "The War on Drugs Is Working," *The Progressive*, June 1, 2018 (https://progressive.org/magazine/the-war-on-drugs-is-working/)

Haagh, Louise (2012) "Democracy, public finance, and property rights in economic stability: How more horizontal capitalism upscales freedom for all," *Polity* 44:4

Hahn, Heather (2018) "What Research Tells Us about Work Requirements," Urban Institute (https://www.urban.org/sites/default/files/publication/98425/what_research_t ells_us_about_work_requirements_19.pdf)

Hammond, Samuel (2017) "The Pro-work Case for Universal Basic Income," Niskanen Center (https://niskanencenter.org/blog/ubi-pro-work/)

Harari, Yuval Noah (2018) *21 Lessons for the 21st Century*, New York: Spiegel & Grau

Harris, Benjamin H., Eugene Steuerle, and Caleb Quakenbush (2018) "Evaluating Tax Expenditures: Introducing Oversight into Spending Through the Tax Code," Tax Policy Center (https://www.urban.org/sites/default/files/publication/98742/evaluating_tax_ expenditures_introducing_oversight_into_spending_through_the_tax_code_1.p df)

Hodge, Scott A. (2005) "Number of Americans Outside the Income Tax System Continues to Grow, Tax Foundation Fiscal Fact No. 27 (https://taxfoundation.org/number-americans-outside-income-tax-system-continues-grow/)

Holzer, Harry (2019) *Immigration and the U.S. Labor Market: A Look Ahead*, Migration Policy Institute (https://www.migrationpolicy.org/research/immigration-us-labor-market-look-ahead)

Hughes, Chris (2018) *Fair Shot: Rethinking Inequality and How We Earn*, New York: St. Martin's Press

Hughes, James J. (2014) "A Strategic Opening for a Basic Income Guarantee in the Global Crisis Being Created by AI, Robots, Desktop Manufacturing and BioMedicine," *Journal of Evolution and Technology* 24:1 (https://jetpress.org/v24/hughes2.htm)

Hugill, Johnny, and Matija Franklin (2017) "The Wisdom of a Universal Basic Income," Behavioral Scientist (http://behavioralscientist.org/wisdom-universal-basic-income/)

Jaumotte, Florence, Ksenia Koloskova, and Sweta C. Saxena (2016) *Impact of Migration on Income Levels in Advanced Economies*, International Monetary Fund, Spillover Task Force (https://www.imf.org/en/Publications/Spillover-Notes/Issues/2016/12/31/Impact-of-Migration-on-Income-Levels-in-Advanced-Economies-44343)

Kaiser Family Foundation (2021) Health Insurance Marketplace Calculator (https://www.kff.org/interactive/subsidy-calculator-2021/)

Kendi, Ibram X. (2019) *How to Be an Antiracist*, New York: One World

King, Martin Luther (1967) "The Three Evils of Society," transcribed by Ephraim Davis, Address Delivered at the National Conference for New Politics, August 31, 1967 (https://www.scribd.com/doc/134362247/Martin-Luther-King-Jr-The-Three-Evils-of-Society-1967#scribd)

Klein, Ezra (2016) "A universal basic income only makes sense if Americans change how they think about work," *Vox*, June 1, 2016 (https://www.vox.com/2016/6/1/11827024/universal-basic-income)

Kolbert, Elizabeth (2018) "The Psychology of Inequality," *The New Yorker*, January 15, 2018 (https://www.newyorker.com/magazine/2018/01/15/the-psychology-of-inequality)

Lee, Alvin (1971) "I'd Love to Change the World," song lyrics from *A Space in Time* album by Ten Years After, released by Columbia Records

Leonard, Christopher (2022) *The Lords of Easy Money: How the Federal Reserve Broke the American Economy*, New York: Simon & Schuster

Levin, Yuval (2011) "Beyond the Welfare State," *National Affairs*, Spring 2011 (https://nationalaffairs.com/publications/detail/beyond-the-welfare-state)

______ (2014) "A Conservative Governing Vision," *National Review*, May 28, 2014 (https://www.nationalreview.com/2014/05/conservative-governing-vision-yuval-levin/)

Lopez, German (2017) "The new war on drugs," *Vox*, September 13, 2017 (https://www.vox.com/policy-and-politics/2017/9/5/16135848/drug-war-opioid-epidemic)

Lowrey, Annie (2018a) *Give People Money: How a Universal Basic Income Would End Poverty, Revolutionize Work, and Remake the World*, New York: Crown

______ (2018b) "Say Hello to Full Employment," *The Atlantic*, July 6, 2018 (https://www.theatlantic.com/business/archive/2018/07/hello-full-employment/564527/?utm_source=newsletter&utm_medium=email&utm_cam paign=atlantic-daily-newsletter&utm_content=20180706&silverid-ref=NDM2NjAyODQxMjlwS0)

Markovits, Daniel (2019) *The Meritocracy Trap: How America's Foundational Myth Feeds Inequality, Dismantles the Middle Class, and Devours the Elite*, New York: Penguin Press

Marr, Chuck, and Brian Highsmith (2012) *Six Tests for Corporate Tax Reform*, Center on Budget and Policy Priorities (https://www.cbpp.org/sites/default/files/atoms/files/2-28-11tax.pdf)

Marr, Chuck, Chye-Ching Huang, and Joel Friedman (2013) *Tax Expenditure Reform: An Essential Ingredient of Needed Deficit Reduction*, Center on Budget and Policy Priorities (https://www.cbpp.org/sites/default/files/atoms/files/2-27-13tax.pdf)

McIntosh, Steve (2020) *Developmental Politics: How America Can Grow Into a Better Version of Itself*, St. Paul: Paragon House

McKay, Conor, Ethan Pollack, and Alastair Fitzpayne (2019) *Automation and a Changing Economy, Part II: Policies for Shared Prosperity*, Aspen Institute Future of Work Initiative (https://www.aspeninstitute.org/publications/automation-and-a-changing-economy-policies-for-shared-prosperity/)

Millerd, Paul (2018) "Crisis at Work: Why Today's Organizations Are Failing To Unleash Human Potential" (https://think-boundless.com/crisis-at-work-why-todays-organizations-are-failing-to-unleash-human-potential/)

Mitnik, Pablo A., and David B. Grusky (2015) *Economic Mobility in the United States*, The Pew Charitable Trusts and the Russell Sage Foundation (http://www.pewtrusts.org/~/media/assets/2015/07/fsm-irs-report_artfinal.pdf?la=en)

Moon, Thomas Allen (2023) *Payback: Why the Top 1% Must Invest in the Rest and How it Can Renew America*, The Payback Project (https://paybackproject.net/)

Mukunda, Gautam (2012) *Indispensable: When Leaders Really Matter*, Boston: Harvard Business Review Press

Murray, Charles (2016) *In Our Hands: A Plan to Replace the Welfare State*, Washington: The AEI Press

Naidu, Suresh, and Aaron Sojourner (2020) *Employer Power and Employee Skills: Understanding Workforce Training Programs in the Context of Labor Market Power*, Roosevelt Institute (https://rooseveltinstitute.org/publications/employer-power-employee-skills-workforce-training-programs-labor-market-power/)

Neuman, Tricia, Karen Pollitz, and Jennifer Tolbert (2018) "Medicare-for-All and Public Plan Buy-In Proposals: Overview and Key Issues," Kaiser Family Foundation Issue Brief, October 2018 (http://files.kff.org/attachment/Issue-Brief-Medicare-for-All-and-Public-Buy-In-Proposals-Overview-and-Key-Issues)

Neuert, Harrison, et al. (2019) *Work Requirements Don't Work: A behavioral science perspective* (http://www.ideas42.org/wp-content/uploads/2019/04/ideas42-Work-Requirements-Paper.pdf)

Nikiforos, Michalis, Marshall Steinbaum, and Gennaro Zezza (2017) *Modeling the Macroeconomic Effects of a Universal Basic Income*, Roosevelt Institute (https://rooseveltinstitute.org/wp-content/uploads/2020/07/RI-Macroeconomic-Effects-of-UBI-201708.pdf)

Olson, Mancur (1971) *The Logic of Collective Action: Public Goods and the Theory of Groups*, Cambridge: Harvard University Press

______ (1982) *The Rise and Decline of Nations*, New Haven, CT: Yale University Press

Organization for Economic Co-operation and Development (2023) M3 for the United States (https://fred.stlouisfed.org/series/MABMM301USA189S)

Ortega, Francesc (2004) "Immigration and the Survival of the Welfare State," Universitat Pompeu Fabra Economics Working Paper #815, (http://ideas.repec.org/p/upf/upfgen/815.html)

Ortman, Jennifer M., Victoria A. Velkoff, and Howard Hogan (2014) "An Aging Nation: The Older Population in the United States," US Census Bureau (https://www.census.gov/library/publications/2014/demo/p25-1140.html)

Orwell, George ([1949] 1983) *Nineteen Eighty-Four*, New York: Penguin Group

Painter, Anthony, and Chris Thuong (2016) *Creative citizen, creative state: the principled and pragmatic case for a Universal Basic Income*, RSA (https://www.thersa.org/discover/publications-and-articles/reports/basic-income)

Passel, Jeffrey S., and D'Vera Cohn (2017) "Immigration projected to drive growth in U.S. working-age population through at least 2035," Pew Research Center (http://www.pewresearch.org/fact-tank/2017/03/08/immigration-projected-to-drive-growth-in-u-s-working-age-population-through-at-least-2035/)

Paul, Ron (2009) *End the Fed*, New York, NY: Grand Central Publishing

Pearlstein, Steven (2018) *Can American Capitalism Survive?: Why Greed Is Not Good, Opportunity Is Not Equal, and Fairness Won't Make Us Poor*, New York: St. Martin's Press

Petrou, Karen (2021) *Engine of Inequality: The Fed and the Future of Wealth in America*, Hoboken: John Wiley & Sons

Pew Research Center (2022) "Americans' Views of Government: Decades of Distrust, Enduring Support for Its Role" (https://www.pewresearch.org/politics/wp-content/uploads/sites/4/2022/06/PP_2022.06.06_views-of-government_REPORT.pdf)

Piketty, Thomas (2017) *Capital in the Twenty-first Century*, trans. Arthur Goldhammer, Cambridge: Harvard University Press

_____ (2020) *Capital and Ideology*, trans. Arthur Goldhammer, Cambridge: Harvard University Press

Piketty, Thomas, Emmanuel Saez, and Gabriel Zucman (2018) "Distributional National Accounts: Methods and Estimates for the United States," Quarterly Journal of Economics 133:2 (http://gabriel-zucman.eu/files/PSZ2018QJE.pdf)

Pope, Chris (2018) "Degenerate Federalism," *National Review*, May 28, 2018 (https://www.nationalreview.com/magazine/2018/05/28/amazon-hq2-cities-shifting-cost-federal-government/)

Porter, Eduardo (2012) "Numbers Tell of Failure in Drug War," *The New York Times*, July 3, 2012 (https://www.nytimes.com/2012/07/04/business/in-rethinking-the-war-on-drugs-start-with-the-numbers.html)

Powell, Michael (2006) "U.S. Immigration Debate is a Road Well Traveled," *Washington Post*, May 8, 2006, (http://www.washingtonpost.com/wp-dyn/content/article/2006/05/07/AR2006050700721.html?nav=hcmodule)

Rawls, John (1971) *A Theory of Justice*, Cambridge, MA: Harvard University Press

RealClear Politics (2023) Congressional Job Approval (https://realclearpolitics.com/epolls/other/congressional_job_approval-903.html#)

Reinhart, R.J. (2018) "Public Split on Basic Income for Workers Replaced by Robots," The Gallup Organization, February 26, 2018 (https://news.gallup.com/poll/228194/public-split-basic-income-workers-replaced-robots.aspx)

Richardson, Steven O. (2011) *The Political Economy of Bureaucracy*, New York: Routledge

_____ (2013) "Entitlement Reform: From Tangled Web to Safety Net," *Basic Income Studies* 8:1

Rickards, James (2014) *The Death of Money: The Coming Collapse of the International Monetary System*, New York: Penguin Group

Roberts, Yvonne, et al. (2016) "I, Daniel Blake: Ken Loach and the scandal of Britain's benefits system," *The Guardian*

(https://www.theguardian.com/film/2016/sep/11/i-daniel-blake-ken-loach-director-film-movie-benefits-system)

Rogers, Brishen (2017) "Basic Income in a Just Society," *Boston Review*, May 15, 2017 (http://bostonreview.net/forum/brishen-rogers-basic-income-just-society)

Rouanet, Louis (2017) "How Central Banking Increased Inequality," Mises Wire, August 15, 2017 (https://mises.org/library/how-central-banking-increased-inequality)

Russell, Bertrand (1932) "In Praise of Idleness," Harper's Magazine, October 1932 (https://harpers.org/archive/1932/10/in-praise-of-idleness/)

Santens, Scott (2015) "Universal Basic Income Will Likely Increase Social Cohesion," *Huffington Post*, December 6, 2017 (https://www.huffingtonpost.com/scott-santens/universal-basic-income-wi_b_8354072.html)

______ (2018) "It's Time for Technology to Serve all Humankind with Unconditional Basic Income," Medium Basic Income (https://medium.com/basic-income/its-time-for-technology-to-serve-all-humankind-with-unconditional-basic-income-e46329764d28)

Sawhill, Isabel (2018) "What the forgotten Americans really want—and how to give it to them," Brookings Institution (https://www.brookings.edu/longform/what-the-forgotten-americans-really-want-and-how-to-give-it-to-them/)

Schuetz, Jenny (2018) "Nine rules for better housing policy," Brookings Institution (https://www.brookings.edu/blog/the-avenue/2018/05/02/nine-rules-for-better-housing-policy/)

Semuels, Alana (2015) "When the Government Tells Poor People How to Live," *The Atlantic*, December 14, 2015 (https://www.theatlantic.com/business/archive/2015/12/paternalism/420210/)

______ (2018) "The Internet Is Enabling a New Kind of Poorly Paid Hell," *The Atlantic*, January 23, 2018 (https://www.theatlantic.com/amp/article/551192/?utm_source=twb&_twitter_impression=true)

Sen, Amartya (1999) *Development as Freedom*, New York: Anchor Books

Shaefer, H. Luke (2016) "Precarious Work and the Employment-based Safety Net," Stanford Social Innovation Review, January 20, 2016 (https://ssir.org/the_hidden_lives_of_americas_poor_and_middle_class/entry/precarious_work_and_the_employment_based_safety_net)

Shaefer, H. Luke, and Kathryn Edin (2018) "Welfare Reform and the Families It Left Behind," *Pathways*, Winter 2018 (https://inequality.stanford.edu/sites/default/files/Pathways_Winter2018_Families-Left-Behind.pdf)

Shaefer, H. Luke, et al. (2018) "A Universal Child Allowance: A Plan to Reduce Poverty and Income Instability Among Children in the United States," The Russell Sage Foundation Journal of the Social Sciences 4:2 (https://www.jstor.org/stable/pdf/10.7758/rsf.2018.4.2.02.pdf)

Shapiro, Robert (2018) "The new economics of jobs is bad news for working-class Americans—and maybe for Trump," Brookings Fixgov January 16, 2018 (https://www.brookings.edu/blog/fixgov/2018/01/16/the-new-economics-of-jobs-is-bad-news-for-working-class-americans-and-maybe-for-trump/)

Sheahen, Alan (2012) *Basic Income Guarantee: Your Right to Economic Security*, New York: Palgrave Macmillan

Shell, Ellen Ruppel (2018) *The Job: Work and its Future in a Time of Radical Change*, New York: Currency

Slattery, Cailin, and Owen Zidar (2020) "Evaluating State and Local Business Tax Incentives," *Journal of Economic Perspectives* 34:2 (https://www.jstor.org/stable/pdf/26913186.pdf?refreqid=excelsior%3A628957fde7f8b12fcc39cbc6712e77a7&ab_segments=&origin=&initiator=&acceptTC=1)

Smith, Adam ([1759] 1982) *The Theory of Moral Sentiments*, eds. D.D. Raphael and A.L. MacFie, Indianapolis: Liberty Fund, Inc.

Solzhenitsyn, Aleksandr Isaevich (1974) *The Gulag Archipelago, 1918-1956: an experiment in literary investigation, I-II*, New York: Harper & Row

Standing, Guy (2016) *The Corruption of Capitalism: Why Rentiers Thrive and Work Does Not Pay*, London: Biteback Publishing

Statista (2022) "Forecasted U.S. national health expenditure as percentage of GDP from 2021 to 2031, (https://www.statista.com/statistics/934320/us-health-expenditure-as-percent-of-gdp-forecast/)

______ (2023) "Total interest expense on debt held by the public of the United States from 2012 to 2022," (https://www.statista.com/statistics/246439/interest-expense-on-us-public-debt/)

Stern, Andy (2016) *Raising the Floor: How a Universal Basic Income Can Renew our Economy and Rebuild the American Dream*, New York: Public Affairs

Stewart, Matthew (2018) "The 9.9 Percent Is the New American Aristocracy," *The Atlantic*, June 2018 (https://www.theatlantic.com/magazine/archive/2018/06/the-birth-of-a-new-american-aristocracy/559130/?utm_source=newsletter&utm_medium=email&utm_campaign=atlantic-daily-newsletter&utm_content=20180516&silverid-ref=NDM2NjAyODQxMjIwwS0)

Stockman, David A. (2013) *The Great Deformation: The Corruption of Capitalism in America*, New York: Public Affairs

______ (2016) *Trumped! A Nation on the Brink of Ruin... and How to Bring It Back*, Baltimore: Laissez Faire Books

______ (2019) *Peak Trump: The Undrainable Swamp and the Fantasy of MAGA*, Contra Corner Press

______ (2023) *The Great Money Bubble: Protect Yourself from the Coming Inflation Storm*, West Palm Beach: Humanix Books

Strain, Michael R. (2016) "Universal basic income won't make America great again, either," *The Washington Post*, April 4, 2016 (https://www.washingtonpost.com/posteverything/wp/2016/04/04/universal-basic-income-wont-make-america-great-again-either/?utm_term=.782234955c6e)

Tam, Stephanie (2020) "How Immigrants Drive Entrepreneurship and Innovation," *Behavioral Scientist*, January 27, 2020 (https://behavioralscientist.org/how-immigrants-drive-entrepreneurship-invention-innovation/)

Tanner, Michael (2015) *The Pros and Cons of a Guaranteed National Income*, Cato Institute Policy Analysis Number 773 (https://object.cato.org/sites/cato.org/files/pubs/pdf/pa773.pdf)

Tax Policy Center (2017a) "Effective Marginal Tax Rates on Wages, Salaries, and Capital Income, By Expanded Cash Income Percentile, 2017" (https://www.taxpolicycenter.org/model-estimates/baseline-effective-marginal-tax-rates-march-2017/t17-0066-effective-marginal-tax)

______ (2017b) "Historical Highest Marginal Income Tax Rates" (https://www.taxpolicycenter.org/statistics/historical-highest-marginal-income-tax-rates)

______ (2022) Tax Policy Center Briefing Book, "What are the sources of revenue for the federal government," (https://www.taxpolicycenter.org/briefing-book/what-are-sources-revenue-federal-government)

Telesford, Imani, et al. (2023) "How has U.S. spending on healthcare changed over time?," Peterson-Kaiser Health System Tracker (https://www.healthsystemtracker.org/chart-collection/u-s-spending-healthcare-changed-time/#Total%20national%20health%20expenditures,%20US%20$%20Billions,%201970-2021)

Thompson, Derek (2019) "Workism Is Making Americans Miserable," *The Atlantic*, February 24, 2019 (https://www.theatlantic.com/ideas/archive/2019/02/religion-workism-making-americans-miserable/583441/)

Ton, Zeynep (2023) *The Case for Good Jobs: How Great Companies Bring Dignity, Pay & Meaning to Everyone's Work*, Boston: Harvard Business Review Press

US Census Bureau (2021) Historical Reported Voting Rates (https://www.census.gov/library/visualizations/time-series/demo/voting-historical-time-series.html)

______ (2022a) Median Household Income in the United States (https://www.census.gov/library/visualizations/2022/comm/median-household-income.html)

______ (2022b) Historical Income Tables: Households, Table H-12. Household by Number of Earners by Median and Mean Income, All Races (https://www2.census.gov/programs-surveys/cps/tables/time-series/historical-income-households/h12ar.xlsx)

US Congressional Budget Office (2012) *Effective Marginal Tax Rates for Low- and Moderate-Income Workers* (http://www.cbo.gov/sites/default/files/cbofiles/attachments/11-15-2012-MarginalTaxRates.pdf)

______ (2019) *The Effects on Employment and Family Income of Increasing the Federal Minimum Wage* (https://www.cbo.gov/system/files/2019-07/CBO-55410-MinimumWage2019.pdf)

______ (2023a) "Discretionary Spending in Fiscal Year 2022: An Infographic," March 28, 2023 (https://www.cbo.gov/publication/58890)

______ (2023b) *The 2023 Long-Term Budget Outlook* (https://www.cbo.gov/publication/59331)

US Constitution (1787) (https://www.archives.gov/founding-docs/constitution-transcript)

US Department of Agriculture (2023) Food and Nutrition Service
(https://www.fns.usda.gov/snap/supplemental-nutrition-assistance-program-snap)

US Department of Education (2020) *Digest of Education Statistics: 2020*, National Center for Education Statistics, Table 106.70
(https://nces.ed.gov/programs/digest/d20/tables/dt20_106.70.asp)

US Department of Health and Human Services (2022a) *The 2022 Annual Report of the Boards of Trustees of the Federal Hospital Insurance and Federal Supplemental Medical Insurance Trust Funds* (https://www.cms.gov/files/document/2022-medicare-trustees-report.pdf)

______ (2022b) Administration for Children and Families, Office of Family Assistance (https://www.acf.hhs.gov/ofa/programs/tanf/about)

______ (2023) U.S. Federal Poverty Guidelines used to Determine Financial Eligibility for Certain Federal Programs (https://aspe.hhs.gov/topics/poverty-economic-mobility/poverty-guidelines)

US Department of Labor, Bureau of Labor Statistics (2023a) Consumer Price Index for All Urban Consumers: Purchasing Power of the Consumer Dollar
(https://fred.stlouisfed.org/series/CUUR0000SA0R)

______ (2023b) Weekly and Hourly Earnings from the Current Population Survey
(https://fred.stlouisfed.org/series/LEU0252881600A)

US Department of the Treasury (2020a) *Internal Revenue Service Statistics of Income,* Individual Statistical Tables by Filing Status, Table 1.2, Tax Year 2020
(https://www.irs.gov/statistics/soi-tax-stats-individual-statistical-tables-by-filing-status#_grp1)

______ (2020b) *Internal Revenue Service Statistics of Income,* Individual Statistical Tables by Size of Adjusted Gross Income, Table 1.4, Tax Year 2020
(https://www.irs.gov/statistics/soi-tax-stats-individual-statistical-tables-by-size-of-adjusted-gross-income)

______ (2022a) *The State of Labor Market Competition,*
(https://home.treasury.gov/system/files/136/State-of-Labor-Market-Competition-2022.pdf)

______ (2022b) *Internal Revenue Service Publication 596 Earned Income Credit*
(https://www.irs.gov/pub/irs-pdf/p596.pdf)

______ (2023) *Tax Expenditures* (https://home.treasury.gov/policy-issues/tax-policy/tax-expenditures)

US Federal Housing Finance Agency (2023) All-Transactions House Price Index for the United States (https://fred.stlouisfed.org/series/USSTHPI/)

US Office of Management and Budget (2023) *Budget of the United States Government,* Historical Tables (https://www.govinfo.gov/app/collection/budget/2023/BUDGET-2023-TAB)

US Social Security Administration (2007) Research Note #20: The Social Security Trust Funds and the Federal Budget (https://www.ssa.gov/history/BudgetTreatment.html)

______ (2022a) *The 2022 Annual Report of the Board of Trustees of the Federal Old-Age and Survivors Insurance and Federal Disability Insurance Trust Funds* (https://www.ssa.gov/OACT/tr/2022/tr2022.pdf)

______ (2022b) *Annual Statistical Supplement, 2022*, Old-Age, Survivors, and Disability Insurance, Table 4.A3 https://www.ssa.gov/policy/docs/statcomps/supplement/2022/4a.pdf)

______ (2022c) *Annual Statistical Supplement, 2022*, Supplemental Security Income, Table 7A (https://www.ssa.gov/policy/docs/statcomps/supplement/2022/7a.pdf)

Watts, Alan (2015) "Money, Guilt, and the Machine," lecture transcribed by Scott Santens (http://www.scottsantens.com/yeah-but-who-is-going-to-pay-for-it-basic-income-alan-watts)

Weissman, Jordan (2016) "The Failure of Welfare Reform: How Bill Clinton's signature legislative achievement tore America's safety net," *Slate,* June 1, 2016 (http://www.slate.com/articles/news_and_politics/moneybox/2016/06/how_welfare_reform_failed.html)

Wolkomir, Elizabeth, and Stacy Dean (2018) "Will Chairman Conaway's SNAP Proposal Match His Rhetoric?," Center on Budget and Policy Priorities, April 12, 2018 (https://www.cbpp.org/sites/default/files/atoms/files/4-11-18fa.pdf)

Yandle, Bruce (1983) "Bootleggers and Baptists-The Education of a Regulatory Economist," *Regulation* 7:3 (https://object.cato.org/sites/cato.org/files/serials/files/regulation/1983/5/v7n3-3.pdf)

Yang, Andrew (2018) *The War on Normal People: The Truth About America's Disappearing Jobs and Why Universal Basic Income is Our Future,* New York: Hachette Books

Zewde, Naomi, et al. (2021) *A Guaranteed Income for the 21st Century,* The New School Institute on Race and Political Economy (https://kirwaninstitute.osu.edu/sites/default/files/Guaranteed%20Income%20for%20the%2021st%20Century.pdf)

Index

www.ingramcontent.com/pod-product-compliance
Lightning Source LLC
Chambersburg PA
CBHW072259260726
48658CB00004BA/1277